W9-CBM-908

THE BRITISH LIBRARY
writers' lives

Joseph Conrad

an end.

It was a great peace, *as if the earth had been one grave* ~~but I was~~ *and for a time I stood there.* Think mostly of the living who buried in its ~~remot~~ ~~places are lost~~ to life as we conceive it ~~yet~~ ~~those~~ ~~dying are not freed from~~ ~~its tragic or grotesque miseries~~ places out of the knowledge of mankind ~~st~~ are fated to share in its tragic or grotesque miseries. In its noble struggles too — who ~~kn~~ The human heart is ~~great~~ *vast* enough to ~~conte~~ ~~all the world and carry~~ ~~the burden all its~~ ~~all its soluble and insoluble problems in~~ ~~unspeakable solitudes~~ *every desert of its choice* ~~beyond the reach of~~ ~~human voices~~

all the world and strong enough to carry ~~over~~ its palpitating walls into the most dumb ~~an~~ deserted wilderness all the *worlds* unrest, all ~~its p~~ ~~rities~~ and — I verily believe — the solution of ~~its~~ innumerable problems. It is ~~strong~~ *valiant* enough bear the burden but where is the courage ~~tha~~ ~~would cast it off~~!

~~I suppose I must have fallen in~~ *lost*
~~sentimental mood for I stood there a lon~~
~~time till at last the sense of utter solitud~~
~~got hold of me and made me almost f~~

THE BRITISH LIBRARY
writers' lives

Joseph Conrad

CHRIS FLETCHER

OXFORD
UNIVERSITY PRESS

FOR CHRIS BARLOW

≈ Contents

8658

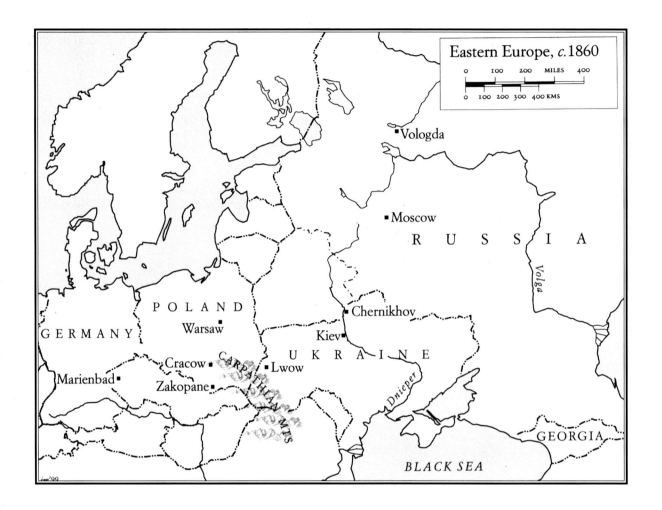

〰 *'My Hazardous Childhood'*

On a fine day in May 1869 a solemn crowd of thousands led by an eleven-year-old boy moved through the streets of Cracow to the mournful tolling of bells. The occasion was the funeral of Apollo Korzeniowski, Polish patriot and revolutionary; the boy, his only son. The young Jozef Teodor Konrad Korzeniowski, noble, exile and now orphan, had already led an extraordinary life. How much more extraordinary that after many years sailing the seas, he would emerge as Joseph Conrad, an Englishman and one of the world's greatest writers.

Apollo Korzeniowski, Conrad's father.

Yale University Library

Conrad was born in the Ukraine on 3 December 1857, to parents whose families had long been involved in the turbulent history of their country. Poland had ceased to be one of the foremost powers in Europe in 1795, when it was divided up between foreign powers, among which Russia was the most important. Apollo, descended from an ancient noble family, inherited a revolutionary ardour which manifested itself in numerous uprisings against the Russians. His father's lands were confiscated in one such rebellion, that of 1830, when he was eleven years old.

All the resentment inspired by his country's burden, his family's oppression and his own humble position as an estate's manager gathered force and focus as Apollo himself entered fatherhood. In a christening song 'To My son born in the 85th year of Muscovite oppression', he grimly laments of the infant Conrad that 'You are without land, without love, without country, without people, while Poland - your mother - is in her grave'.

Ewalina Bobrowska, Conrad's mother.

Yale University Library

Conrad's mother came from a more moderate background. The Bobrowskis, although patriots, had always measured the consequences of their political and military actions a little more carefully than the Korzeniowskis. For this reason Ewalina brought to their marriage, on 8 May 1856, not only considerable beauty and warmth of personality, but a substantial dowry and the security of a family which had managed to retain at least some of its lands. Not surprisingly, her parents regarded Apollo with suspicion; according to her brother, Tadeusz, their mother found him 'irresponsible and erratic in behaviour', while their father thought him unpractical and lazy.

The concerns of Ewalina's parents proved well founded. Before long, Apollo had managed to lose, in addition to his own money, his wife's nine thousand roubles in silver. After a further three years he lost patience with his tedious estate work and took his family to Zytomierz. The revolutionary winds which gathered in this province soon fanned the flame of his smouldering political sentiments and the dangerous, clandestine world of radical patriotism claimed him as its own. In 1861 he was drawn to Warsaw, an even more volatile city still reeling from the violent suppression of two vast patriotic demonstrations. Apollo was by now an established author and translator, and his declared aim was to start a literary magazine. His more fervent intent revealed itself as he emerged a charismatic revolutionary leader.

Meanwhile, Conrad remained in the Ukraine on his grandmother's estate with his mother. Ewa's letters to Apollo reveal a loving wife and mother yearning for her husband's return yet keenly aware of the dangers which rendered this impossible.

Her son's earliest extant piece of writing (appended to one of her letters) echoes her sadness, its description of trivial frustrations and hopes providing an unwittingly ironic commentary on the dark scenes played out on a larger stage: 'Daddy, I am fine here, I run about the garden - but I don't like it much when the mosquitos bite. As soon as the rain stops I will come to you.' Despite this forlorn situation, Ewa wrote to Apollo that 'Konradek is a good boy: it is amazing how God lets him win people's hearts'. His grandmother concurred: 'no pen could catch and render all the shades of goodness that child has in him ... I suspect that our dear Konradzio will grow into an exceptional man with a great heart.'

Ewa and Conrad eventually risked travelling to Warsaw, where the family barely had time to celebrate their reunion. The authorities finally caught up with Apollo, who was arrested for clandestine political activities and sentenced to seven months in prison. The traumatized Ewa, increasingly weak from the symptoms of tuberculosis, described to friends how her husband was taken on 20 October, just after the clocks had struck midnight: 'We were both awake: he writing, I reading. Six minutes after the door-bell had rung he was gone from the house.' Among other dressed-up charges, Apollo was accused of instigating brawls in coffee shops. Although spared imprisonment, Ewa herself did not escape censure. She had, for example, distributed mourning dress to the colleagues of fallen protestors. No doubt Conrad's entreaties for such an outfit rendered even him a criminal in the eyes of the authorities.

Joseph Conrad in 1862, with whip.

British Library

On his release from prison Apollo was sentenced to exile. Conrad and his mother barely survived the gruelling journey through the vast Russian wastes to the remote town of Vologda. Ewa's tubercular condition and her son's fever were treated along the way by applying leeches to draw the blood. There was little improvement in their comfort when they arrived on 16 June 1862. The log house in which the family would stay was depressingly spartan and, like the others which huddled around it, quite unable to defend its occupants from the ravages of the weather. Apollo complained to friends that 'even when the stoves are red-hot, after several days of frost a white moss appears in the corners of the warmest of dwellings'. It was so very cold he continued, managing to summon a certain amount of grim humour, that 'if the Pharisees, having tortured Christ to death, buried him in Vologda, there would be no need for seals or guards - the act of our redemption would still be lying in cold storage'.

Redemption of some kind was what they sought, yet several months into the unrelenting tedium of their isolation the only news heard by the exiles was that a major Polish insurrection had been mercilessly crushed by the Russians. Their relatives were among the casualties. 'We are stunned by despair', wrote Apollo. Conrad, in a gesture of sympathy and defiance, sent a photograph of himself 'to my beloved Grandma who helped me send cakes to my poor Daddy in prison', signing it 'grandson, Pole, Catholic, nobleman - 6 July 1863 - Konrad.' He now knew that the benign supports upon which he had unquestioningly depended could be threatened and lost. His mother, her illness deepening, would emerge from this period in his memories 'with more distinctness than a mere loving, wide-browed, silent, protecting presence'.

In an act of mercy which came not a moment too soon, the family were allowed by the authorities to move further south to the more hospitable Chernikhov. From here Conrad and his mother were granted a further temporary concession and travelled to the Bobrowski estate 120 miles away in Nowofastow. Conrad played for three sun-drenched summer months in the 'great unfenced fields' with his cousin, 'a delightful, quick tempered little girl'. He barely noticed the comings and goings of the sober-faced doctors attending his mother. The summer disappeared all too quickly before mother and son were obliged to return to Chernikhov. Conrad recalled the moment of their enforced departure: 'the ... shabby travelling carriage with four post-horses standing before the long front of the house with its eight columns ... on the steps, groups of servants, a few relations, one or two friends from the nearest neighbourhood, a perfect silence, on all the faces an air of sober concentration.'

Back in Chernikhov Ewa's illness drew towards its sad conclusion, despite her distraught husband's pleas for better doctors and a healthier place of exile. Apollo sank into a 'black sorrow', lamenting of his wife that 'only occasionally a stronger embrace for myself or Konradek tells of her courage'. Ewa died on 18 April 1865. Apollo haunted her grave, confessing to a friend that 'my deepest beliefs are shaken; doubts consume all my thoughts'. He took what solace he could in his son, making 'all necessary sacrifices today to ensure his tomorrow'. Keen that Conrad should receive an education, he sold a desk of which Ewa had been particularly fond in order to raise enough money for textbooks. Despite such efforts, he was acutely aware of the emotional dangers attending his son's strange and miserable situation: 'Poor child', he wrote in a letter, 'he does not not know what a contemporary playmate is; he looks at the decrepitude of my sadness and who knows if that sight does not make his young heart wrinkled or his awakening soul grizzled.'

Apollo and Conrad immersed themselves in literature and learning in their lonely house on the edge of town. This provided not only a temporary distraction from grief, but vitally needed income from Apollo's translation work. The young boy later recalled clambering, still in mourning dress, onto his father's chair, to look at his translation of Shakespeare's *Two Gentlemen of Verona*. For his audacity he was teasingly made to read it aloud. Conrad was used to this practice: a few weeks earlier he had read from his father's translation of Victor Hugo's novel, *Toilers of the Sea*. Perhaps it was these words which first started to shape his dual destiny as seaman and writer.

Apollo, his own health now declining, confessed in a letter that 'I teach and demand too much and the little one, seeing nobody, burrows too deeply into books'. His son, precociously well read and now able to speak French, was therefore sent to stay on the Bobrowski estate. His return to Chernikhov in the autumn was short-lived. Conrad had begun to suffer from the vague illness which would recur throughout his childhood years and which seems to have been as much a nervous as a physical complaint. He journeyed to Kiev to see specialists and then, on their advice, went once again to Nowofastow. Despite the love poured upon him by his grandmother and uncle, and the opportunity to play with those his own age, he missed his father terribly.

Conrad and Apollo were reunited in the autumn of 1867 in Lwow, the capital of the Austrian part of Poland. Apollo had been permitted to travel there and the more liberal atmosphere went some way towards lightening his depression. Even so, he was remembered by an elderly neighbour as a 'man ruined both physically and mentally by suffering. Pale, dark-haired with a long beard, extremely wan and sad'. He remained fiercely protective of his son, in whom he increasingly saw resemblances to Ewa, and whom he described to a friend as 'the only strength that keeps me on this earth'.

Conrad was not allowed to attend the local school and sought companionship and adventure more in literature than in the things around him. The few friends he made were obliged to enter this escapist world. One recalled a 'strange boy' who

> 'told us - his play mates - the most extraordinary stories. They were always of the sea and ships and far-away countries ... they were weird and fantastic almost beyond belief, but in the way he told them they seemed to us actual happenings. The power of weaving tales - tales that literally seemed to lie before one's eyes - was born in him.'

Another female friend remembered a 'little tyrant' directing his own patriotic plays in which 'large cardboard boxes served as stage settings' and 'the breaking of chairs and stools' accompanied fierce battles between the insurgents and their Muscovite enemies. 'And as to loving', wrote Apollo, 'he loves those whom I point out to him as worthy'.

The eleven-year-old was once again uprooted when father and son moved to Cracow. Yet all Apollo's literary and political aspirations in that important city were cruelly undercut within months of their arrival; as his father's illness took hold, the oppressive atmosphere of the old house bore down upon the child with a dark gravity he would never forget:

> *'There, in a large drawing-room, panelled and bare, with heavy cornices and a lofty ceiling, in a little oasis of light made by two candles in a desert of dusk, I sat at a little table to worry and ink myself all over till the task of my homework was done ... finished, I would have nothing to do but sit and watch the awful stillness of the sick room flow out through the closed door and coldly enfold my scared heart.'*

Tadeusz Bobrowski Conrad's uncle and guardian. Conrad remembered him as 'the keeper of an inexhaustible treasure of clear thought and warm feeling.'

British Library

Apollo died on 23 May 1869, leaving behind a child so hollowed out by grief he would later confess that 'I don't think I found a single tear to shed'.

It would take a strong and determined man to meet the challenge of Conrad's upbringing in the next few years. Such a man was Tadeusz Bobrowski, 'the keeper', in his nephew's later words, of 'an inexhaustible and noble treasure of clear thought and warm feeling'. Photographs of Bobrowski show a powerful and shrewd-looking man, unlikely to suffer fools gladly. A pragmatist, he had always been sceptical of his brother-in-law, regretting his generous allocation of Korzentiowski 'romanticism'. He was, however, sensitive to the great love Conrad had borne him and assured him in writing that 'you know that the whole affection we felt for your Parents we now bestow upon you'. The consoling letter goes

Joseph Conrad

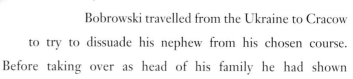

'An air of slight haughtiness'
- Conrad in 1873.

British Library

on to address the boy's erratic education: 'not that which is easy and attractive must be the object of your studies but that which is useful, although sometimes difficult'. Bobrowski's worries ran deeper still. His concerns about Conrad's state of mind are revealed in his warning that he should strive to avoid 'giving way to feelings and thoughts which are not really proper to your age'.

Conrad remained in Cracow, where a place was found for him in a boarding house. His grandmother Teofila remained in the city to keep an eye on him until December, when Stefan Buszczynski, his father's literary executor, became his guardian. Conrad's education had been too patchy to allow him to enter normal schooling, and a twenty-three year old medical student, Adam Pulman, was appointed his private tutor. A brief summer holiday in the Carpathian Mountains did little to help his health, which remained frail, and in December 1870 Teofila returned, to remain with him for the next three years.

In the summer of 1873, Conrad went touring through Europe with Pulman. It was while walking in the lonely Swiss Furca Pass, the sun sinking in the sky that he apparently experienced something like an epiphany. Out of nowhere, a purposefully striding Englishman passed them on the track. Conrad later pondered whether the man was 'in the mystic ordering of common events the ambassador of my future, sent out to turn the scale at a critical moment on top of an Alpine pass'. He had been increasingly preoccupied with the idea of going to sea. This traveller's air of dauntless enthusiasm helped him to focus upon a course of action which must have seemed all the more appealing after his first view of salt water, from the shore of the Lido in Venice.

Bobrowski travelled from the Ukraine to Cracow to try to dissuade his nephew from his chosen course. Before taking over as head of his family he had shown considerable talent as a lawyer. This career, or that of an engineer, technician, or doctor, were those which he hoped Conrad might now pursue. When all his arguments failed, he resorted to sterner measures and Conrad was sent to a boarding house in Lwow for orphans.

Conrad hated the boarding house, being unused to rules, academic discipline or the company of those his own age. The city itself must have stirred up sad memories of the time he had spent there with his father six years earlier. The same girl who recalled the chair-smashing frivolities of his first stay had difficulty recognising him on his return: 'he had grown taller, his hair was long, brushed back, a trace of down announced an incipient moustache. He was in the habit of screwing up his eyes and looking through narrow slits. It gave him an air of slight haughtiness.' A photograph of 1873 shows a handsome face, the expression half imperious, half wistful, rather proud, yet sensitive too. A distant relative involved in the running of the house later confirmed what many were beginning to realise; Conrad was developing into a frustrated and frustrating teenager:

> *'Intellectually well developed, he hated the rigours of school, which tired and bored him; he used to say that he had a great talent and would become a great writer. This, coupled with a sarcastic smile on his face and frequent critical remarks on everything, provoked surprise in his teachers and ridicule among his colleagues. He liked always to be untrammelled and at school, at home, or on a visit preferred to lounge rather than sit.'*

Not everything provoked Conrad's disdain and cynicism. Evoking 'the beautiful Antonia', the feisty heroine of his epic novel *Nostromo*, he later confessed:

> *'I have modelled her on my first love. How we, a band of tallish schoolboys, the chums of her two brothers, how we used to look up to that girl just out of the schoolroom herself ... I was not the only one in love with her; but it was I who had to hear oftenest her scathing criticism of my levities ... or stand the brunt of her austere, unanswerable invective. She did not quite understand - but never mind.'*

Commentators have suggested various identities for this girl, the most likely being Janina Taube, later Baroness Janina de Brunnow.

Conrad must have presented an interesting case for Pulman's growing medical knowledge. In the summer of 1874 the tutor was once again pressed into service, taking his student on holiday in an attempt to alleviate the severe migraines which made further study impossible. Before they set off, he affectionately warned him: 'I shall be in a jovial mood ... so you will have to comply with my disposition, abandon illness and sadness in Lwow, and, apart from a small supply of books, you must bring a considerable amount of willingness to jump, run around, go for strenuous walks, show good appetite, etc., etc.' Pulman had, in fact, grown close to Conrad and had some insight into his dormant genius: 'I expect my pupil not to put me to shame and, eventually to grow up to be a spendid man', he continued, 'So although your head may ache, hold it high.'

As he entered the next stage of his life, Conrad lost touch with Pulman. But he didn't forget him altogether, later recalling the day 'when on the deck of a ship moored in Calcutta, I opened a letter telling me of the end of an enviable existence ... How short his years and how clear his vision!' According to some sources, Pulman had died while working as a doctor, and was much loved and mourned by the poor and dispossessed to whom he had decided to dedicate his life. Conrad wondered, perhaps with a tinge of regret and shame, 'what greater reward in ambition, honour and conscience could he have hoped to win for himself when, on the top of the Furca Pass, he bade me look well to the end of my opening life'.

In the autumn of 1874 Bobrowski finally surrendered his claims on Conrad's better judgement and let him go to sea. Looking back on his decision, Conrad would write that 'the part of the inexplicable should be allowed for in appraising the conduct of men in a world where no explanation is final'. Despite this claim, less mysterious motivations for his actions can be entertained. Bobrowski had tried to secure Austrian citizenship for Conrad. His failure to do so had grave implications. As a Russian subject and son of a convict, Conrad was liable to as many as twenty-five years of military service. The sea provided an effective means of escape from this onerous fate.

Other factors may also have made Conrad's decision less surprising and romantic than he later wished it might appear. He had not shown himself to be a good student in the conventional sense, and his academic future looked distinctly unpromising. Perhaps a physical career would be for the best. His health, also, seemed to demand plenty of clean air, a commodity not lacking at sea. Finally, he was really now too old to depend upon the constant care of long-suffering relatives and friends. It was time he tried to fend for himself.

English ships moored at Calcutta. It was here that Conrad learned of Pulman's death.

*British Library
Mss Eur c174/244*

$\approx$ *'I was a youngster then...'*

'I verily believe', Conrad wrote in *A Personal Record*, 'mine was the only case of a boy of my nationality and antecedents taking a, so to speak, standing jump out of his racial surroundings and associations.' He landed in Marseilles in October 1874 with good French, a rather more modest sense of responsibility, and a larger degree of freedom than he had yet experienced in his eighteen years. He also had, thanks to his uncle, a decent allowance, new clothes, some Polish books, a family photograph and the names of people who could help to establish him in the city.

One such friend was a Pole, Baptistin Solary, a quiet yet cheerful young man. From the moment Conrad woke up after the tiring journey, in his modest hotel near the quays of the old port, Solary introduced him to the life of the city and its inhabitants - including the harbour pilots. Conrad recalled that 'The very first day I ever spent on salt water was by invitation, in a big half-decked pilot-boat, cruising under close reefs on the look out, in misty, blowing weather, for the sails of ships and the smoke of steamers rising out there, beyond the slim and tall Planier lighthouse cutting the line of the wind-swept horizon with a white perpendicular stroke'. He was soon allowed to use the pilots' boats whenever he liked and when ashore appears to have enjoyed the company of their beguiling daughters, 'thick set girls, with pure profiles, glorious masses of black hair arranged with complicated art, dark eyes, and dazzlingly white teeth.'

When not occupied by his role as the 'adopted baby of the pilots of the third company', hanging time around the cafés on the quays, or enjoying the 'revelry going on in the narrow, unspeakable lanes of the Old Town', Conrad spent time with the Delestangs, a wealthy couple who quite possibly encouraged him in his support of the Carlist cause, which aimed to secure the throne of Spain for Don Carlos de Bourbon. It was in the ships owned by Monsieur Delestang, 'with his thin bony nose, and ... perfectly bloodless, narrow physiognomy', that Conrad would first properly sail. His haughty wife seemed fascinated with the callow but handsome young man. She offered him her company on carriage trips around the fashionable parts of the city despite having to endure, according to Conrad himself, 'the prattle of a youngster very full of his new experience amongst strange men and strange sensations'.

Conrad must have felt confused by his position as a poor yet noble exile . Craving the company of tough men who had worked from childhood, he was still glad to fall back upon the sureties of the monied middle classes. What he really needed was an opportunity to escape the equally embarrassing roles of marine mascot or lady's lap dog. A significant step towards this goal was taken when he made his first sea-going voyage in December on the *Mont Blanc*, sailing to Martinique. He was only a passenger but later memories of his first storm at sea reveal a strong sense of somehow belonging to the working life of the ship:

'We, - or, rather, they, for I had hardly had two glimpses of salt water in my life till then - kept her standing off and on all that day, while I listened for the first time with the curiosity of my tender years to the song of the wind in a ship's rigging. The monotonous and vibrating note was destined to grow into the intimacy of the heart, pass into blood and bone, accompany the thoughts and acts of two full decades, remain to haunt like a reproach the peace of the quiet fireside, and enter into the very texture of respectable dreams dreamed safely under a roof of rafter sand tiles.'

On 25 June 1875 the momentous day came when Conrad finally realised his ambitions, sailing this time for the West Indies as an apprentice on the *Mont Blanc*. A year later, having spent the previous six months happily disposing of considerable quantities of his uncle's money in Marseilles (not without reproach), Conrad again embarked for the West Indies on the *Saint-Antoine*, one of Delestang's ships. On his voyage, he forged a friendship with the first mate, the charismatic and swashbuckling Dominic Cervoni. Writing in the future about how this 'astute and ruthless' hero inspired the character of Nostromo in his eponymous masterpiece, Conrad confessed 'it is a real satisfaction to think that in my very young days there must, after all, have been something in me worthy to command that man's half-bitter fidelity, his half-ironic devotion'. Cervoni was the bane of 'Custom-houses and every mortal belonging thereto - scribes, officers, and guardacostas (coastguards)' and it is possible that Conrad was involved with him in gun-running or some other illicit activity during this period.

'Where is here consideration, prudence, and reflection??? Where is here respect for others' - this time my own - peace of mind? Where is here any attempt to soften the impact of the absurdities committed, by prudent and tactful behaviour???' So read Conrad when he returned to Marseilles in February 1877. The stern, chiding letter was from his uncle. 'Let us after these two years go over the past', Bobrowski wrote, going on to demonstrate that Conrad had, by the end of two years, spent the money meant to last for three. His lack of prudence exasperated Bobrowski, who feared that in order to keep pace with his nephew's voracious financial appetite, he would have to 'cut down by half my expenditure on underwear, shoes, clothes, and my personal needs'. Bobrowski's account of Conrad's 'absurdities committed' details his nephew's habit of demanding more money with expensive telegrams, his failure to protect his money from thieves, and a habit of running up debts he could not repay. City life was evidently getting the better of Conrad and Bobrowski therefore advised him to 'try to return to sea as speedily as possible'; nevertheless, by the end of the letter Conrad's profligacy was forgiven, his uncle was even suggesting a joint partnership trading French spirits and Havana cigars.

Bobrowski's advice that Conrad should return speedily to sea was frustrated in part by illness, but also by the resurgence of his 'tendency to fly into a passion' (as his uncle pointed out in another letter). Conrad had fallen out with Delestang, apparently feeling that he had been treated 'too loftily' and without proper regard for his noble status. His immediate land-locked future seemed uncertain, prompting Bobrowski to remark that 'I cannot expect of you in your 19th year to have the maturity of an old man, but I warn you that some day, perhaps soon, you will regret that conversation'. Within a few months these words proved all too true.

Bobrowski became frantically worried about the implications of his nephew remaining in France without the prospect of a berth, exclaiming rhetorically that 'to spend a whole year on land cannot be good either for your health or for practising and perfecting your profession?' Conrad had evidently been making some half-hearted effort to think about his future; options including joining the English merchant fleet ('do you speak English?', enquired his desperate uncle), or living in Switzerland. Bobrowski's next letter seizes upon further possibilities, each aiming to remove the young man from

Marseilles. Travelling to the United States or becoming 'an Admiral in Japan', for example, were better than being further seduced by the questionable charms of the southern city. In truth, Conrad was drifting dangerously towards a crisis. Bobrowski was not able to visit; his amiable and sensible mentor Solary was dead; he was still spending large amounts of money; he had argued recklessly with the one man who could provide him with steady work.

' ... his hand, feeling about his waist, unbuttoned the flap of the leather case, drew the revolver, cocked it, brought it forward pointing at his breast, pulled the trigger, and, with convulsive force, sent the still-smoking weapon hurtling through the air.' Conrad's description of the suicide of the urbane, intellectually audacious and intensely lonely Decoud of Nostromo must have cost him a great deal of courage and pain when he came to write it in late middle age. For early in 1879, isolated, depressed and aged just twenty-one, Conrad also raised a gun to his chest and fired it. Unlike his fictional counterpart, he was not 'swallowed up in the immense indifference of things'. Fate spared him, and the bullet, although coming perilously close, missed his heart.

The events leading up to Conrad's desperate act can be pieced together from a letter of March 1879 from Bobrowski to Stefan Buszczynski, who had enquired after the sensitive young boy once in his charge. Bobrowski had believed Conrad to be on a long voyage, 'when suddenly, amidst all the business at the Kiev Fair in 1878, I received a telegram: "Conrad blessé envoyez argent - arrivez (Conrad wounded send money - come)"'. Arriving in Marseilles after a three-day journey, he quizzed the convalescent. Conrad had been prevented from sailing in any French vessel because of his alien status and the lack of a required permit. Still in possession of the money he had been sent for the voyage by Bobrowski, he foolishly agreed to help to join 'in some enterprise on the coasts of Spain - some kind of contraband!' Initial success encouraged a second investment, all of which was lost. He then borrowed yet more money from a friend, 'Richard Fecht, a most prudent and worthy young man' and, not being able to secure work on any American ships anchored at Villa Franca, eventually resorted to the casino in Monte Carlo. After losing everything, he invited Fecht to tea and 'before his arrival attempts to take his life with a revolver'.

Bobrowski asked of his correspondent that 'this detail remain between us, as I have been telling everyone that he was wounded in a duel'. Conrad himself was keen to perpetuate the myth, richly elaborating upon it in his late novel *The Arrow of Gold*. Here he recreates himself as a Carlist hero involved in risky smuggling escapades with Dominic Cervoni upon a ship called the *Tremolino*. Although Conrad's secret was kept from the world until well after his death, the implications of his act haunted him throughout his life. Over sixteen years later, writing to his aunt assuring her that he had not burnt any of his manuscripts, he took the opportunity to discuss a more profound matter:

> *'One talks like that, but then one lacks the courage. There are those who talk like that of suicide. And then there is always something lacking, sometimes strength, sometimes perseverance, sometimes courage. The courage to succeed or the courage to recognize one's impotence. What remains always cruel and ineradicable is the fear of finality. One temporizes with Fate, one seeks to deceive desire, one tries to play tricks with one's life. Men are always cowards.'*

When Conrad pulled the trigger of his gun he had made sure that the addresses of people close to him were clearly visible and that Fecht was expected. Conforming to the view of suicide set out in the letter to his aunt, Conrad's act fell into the twilight zone between courage and cowardice. He wanted to die, but hoped to be saved. And once saved, his failure to die must have seemed to him - as it later seemed to one of his greatest characters, Lord Jim - just one more humiliating episode in a life patently failing to match up to a young man's romantic conception of himself. His familial, cultural and legal status had been called into question by Delestang and the authorities; no one showed any interest in his marine abilities; he was incapable of earning his own money and had made himself look foolish trying to recover what he had been forced to borrow.

On arriving in Marseilles, Bobrowski had not seen Conrad for four years and was no doubt expecting the worst. What he found was 'not a bad boy, only one who is extremely sensitive, conceited, reserved, and in addition excitable'. He was, in fact, delighted that Conrad drank little except red wine, did not

gamble (his experience in Monte Carlo notwithstanding), was polite, appeared to know his chosen profession and was 'ardent and original' in conversation and thought. All in all, concluded Bobrowski, 'My studies of the Individual have not deprived me of the hope that a real man might still be made of him.'

The conclusion that Conrad had experienced quite enough of Marseilles was probably not a hard one to reach when he and his uncle sat down to decide upon his future. Alternatives may have required a little more thought. Despite the impression later given by Conrad that a career in the English merchant marine was always mysteriously destined, the reasons for his joining were again probably rather more pragmatic. Bobrowski had discovered that the administrative formalities which had hindered Conrad in France were not necessary on English ships. So he joined the *Mavis*, a small steamer bound for Constantinople and then the English port of Lowestoft, where he arrived on 18 June1878.

Lowestoft harbour, Conrad's first experience of England.

National Maritime Museum

23

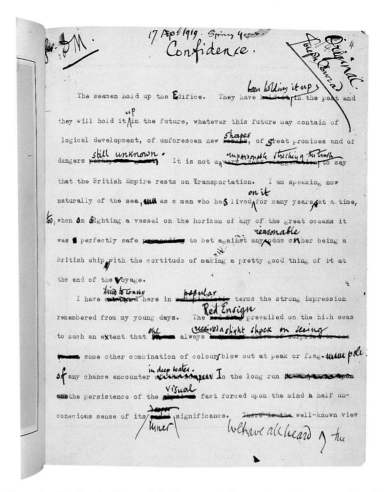

Once in England, Conrad had no mind to stay either on the ship or in Lowestoft, promptly leaving both and wasting his apprentice's fee. His uncle, on discovering his new and unforeseen location (with opportunities for dissipation far exceeding those available in Marseilles), conveyed his outraged opinion in unambiguous terms: 'you travel to London, God knows why, being fully aware that you could not manage by yourself, having nothing and knowing nobody ... really, you have exceeded the limits of stupidity permitted to your age! and you pass beyond the limits of my patience!' Conrad had made straight for the largest and most bewildering city in the world. 'I agreed that you should sail on an English ship but not to your staying in England, not to your travelling to London and wasting my money there!', despaired Bobrowski, before issuing a challenge designed to appeal directly to the young man's heart: 'Think of your parents, of your grandmother, who sacrificed so much for you - remember my sacrifices, my fatherly indulgence and leniency - reform yourself - work

- calculate - be prudent and doggedly pursue your aim and with deeds, not with words
- prove that you deserve my blessing.'

Conrad later remembered the loneliness of walking 'into the great city with something of the feeling of a traveller penetrating into a vast and unexplored wilderness', and Bobrowski's rebuke had the intended effect; by 11 July he had enrolled as an ordinary seaman aboard the *Skimmer of the Seas*, voyaging between Lowestoft and Newcastle where he encountered 'dismal shores ... studded thickly with scaffoldlike, enormous timber structures, whose lofty heads are veiled periodically by the infernal gritty night of a cloud of coal dust'.

Conrad returned to 'that wonder city' of London in October, heading for 'one of those courts hidden away from the charted and navigable streets, lost among the thick growth of houses like a dark pool in the depths of a forest, approached by an inconspicuous archway as if by a secret path'. He was seeking his first really proper 'deep sea' job and, interrupting an elderly shipping agent's meal of mutton chops, 'produced elaborately a series of vocal sounds which must have borne sufficient resemblance to the phonetics of English speech, for his face broke into a smile of comprehension almost at once'. Conrad was granted the berth he had requested earlier in a letter from Lowestoft, which he remembered as his 'very first composition in the English language'.

Circular Quay, Sydney c. 1870, by F. Halsted.

He joined the *Duke of Sutherland*, a one-thousand-ton clipper, bound for Australia. The ship arrived in Sydney after a passage from London of one hundred and nine days. Once there, Conrad wrote to Bobrowski complaining about the uncomfortable conditions on English ships, in spite of which his uncle detected in him 'a liking for his profession'.

One of the jobs for which Conrad was nominated, 'in port, probably on account of my youth, innocence, and pensive habits' was manning the night watch. The role suited him. From the security of the ship he could involve himself vicariously (and inexpensively) in the nocturnal life of the city:

> '*The night humours of the town descended from the street to the waterside in the still watches of the night: larrikins rushing down in bands to settle some quarrell by a stand-up fight, away from the police, in an indistinct ring half hidden by piles of cargo, with the sounds of blows, a groan now and then, the stamping of feet, and the cry of "Time!" rising suddenly above the sinister and excited murmurs; night-prowlers, pursued or pursuing, with a stifled shriek followed by a profound silence, or slinking stealthily alongside like ghosts, and addressing me from the quay below in mysterious tones with incomprehensible propositions.*'

Conrad arrived back in England in October 1879 and wrote excitedly to his uncle of the voyage, hoping, no doubt, to impress him with his growing marine expertise. Bobrowski, however, confessed that he had wanted news of a more personal nature, 'as this is of more interest to me than the direction of the winds that brought you back and which I am ready to regard as favourable if they did not harm you and if you did not suffer from frost-bite'. The voyage had been full of adventure but had been lonely, too. The compulsion to share its details with someone must have been strong. Conrad graphically described it again many years later:

> '*The ship, brought-to and bowing to enormous flashing seas, glistened wet from deck to trucks; her one set sail stood out on a coal-black shape upon the gloomy blueness of the air. I was a youngster then, and suffering from weariness, cold, and imperfect oilskins which let water in at every seam.*

I craved human companionship, and, coming off the poop, took my place by the side of the boatswain (a man whom I did not like) in a comparatively dry spot where at worst we had water only up to our knees.'

The River Thames as Conrad would have known it.

British Library
LB31b. 12776

The last part of the journey involved sailing for the first time up the Thames, a river which exercised a profound effect upon the young mariner and which would continue to do so throughout his life:

'It recalls a jungle by the confused, varied, and impenetrable aspect of the buildings that line the shore, not according to a planned purpose, but as if sprung up by accident from scattered seeds. Like the matted growth of bushes and creepers veiling the silent depths of an unexplored wilderness, they hide the depths of London's infinitely varied, vigorous, seething life ... it is the waterside of watersides.'

The river would famously impose its brooding symbolic presence in perhaps his greatest tale, *Heart of Darkness*, representing, like its tides, the merging of opposites - sea and sky, land and water, past and present, the primitive and the civilised.

Not letting him forget that 'staying on land has always had an inauspicious influence upon you', Bobrowski was relieved when Conrad soon found another position aboard the *Europa*, sailing in the Mediterranean. He remained with the ship for only seven weeks. It seems as though the young sailor, full of himself after his long Australian voyage, had been taken down a peg or two. Certainly, if he had come to his new ship sharing his uncle's assessment of the Mediterranean as nothing more than 'a great lake' he might have expected trouble. Referring in a letter to the 'madman Captain Munro', Bobrowski advised the wounded Conrad that 'we won't change the English, so having to deal with them, we must adapt ourselves'. Such stoicism in the face of cultural adversity was all the more important given that both had by now decided that Conrad should aim for naturalization as an English subject.

Uncle and nephew both had cause to worry about each other's health. Conrad had come down with a bad fever on the *Europa*, whereas Bobrowski was feeling the onset of age. He reassured the young man in a letter of May 1879 that he had not yet taken 'refuge on God's acre', and that in any case Conrad would be informed - at which moment, 'you would say a little prayer and you would become a bit lonelier still in the world - which with you on it would carry on, less one heart and one head that loved you'. Despite Bobrowski's morbidly jocular tone it is possible to detect a genuine and deep concern that his nephew should be starting to put down roots, build something for himself, properly belong. Yet Conrad was not completely alone in London. He had made friends with two men in particular, both with marine backgrounds: Adolf Krieger, a banker and George Hope, a company director (and later the model for the director of companies in *Youth* and *Heart of Darkness*).

Once again without a ship, Conrad had been speculating about joining an American money-making concern. 'Such changes make people become declassé', warned Bobrowski, 'it is much more dignified and sensible to devote your life to and tie your future to a certain profession, putting into it your work and determination'. It was to his uncle's immense relief then, that in June 1880 Conrad passed his exam for the position of second mate. 'It has been a profound pleasure and my first reward', he wrote, delighted that at long last the wanderer had shown himself capable of achieving something palpable. But Conrad's success also delighted Bobrowski in another way, revealing to him that, like Fecht and Solary in France, there were people in the city looking out for and encouraging him: 'that good old fellow of a captain ... that kind-hearted professor Newton ... and those sailors who rejoiced at your success - they all seem very likeable to me at this moment'.

Conrad recalled sitting in the examination, which 'lasted for hours and hours':

> *"This ancient person", I said to myself, terrified, "is so near his grave that he must have lost all notion of time. He is considering this examination in terms of eternity. It is all very well for him. His race is run. But I may find myself coming out of this room into the world of men a stranger, friendless, forgotten by my very landlady, even were I able after this endless experience to remember the way to my hired home."*

Conrad's hired home was, in fact, 6 Dynevor Road, a modest house in Stoke Newington, North London, to which he would return for the next six years between voyages. After his exam success, it took Conrad a while to secure a suitable position. But on 21 August, he sailed as third mate aboard the *Loch Etive* 'one of those iron wool-clippers that the Clyde had floated out in swarms upon the world'. He now occupied a recognised position of responsibility and was even promoted for a while to take the place of the ill second mate. His colleagues appear to have been benevolent if idiosyncratic. He later recalled the deaf captain's passion for borrowing

mirrors from the cabins of the other officers: 'Why? Mystery. We made various surmises. No one will ever know now.' The passage back from Sydney was rough: 'We had seen no sun, moon, or stars for something like seven days ... and the last three days had seen the force of a south-west gale grow from fresh, through strong, to heavy, as the entries in my log book could testify.' Any attempt to conduct duties was hopeless. 'I gave it up, and crawled into my bunk instead, boots and hat on ... to remain in a nightmarish state between waking and sleeping for a couple of hours of so-called rest.'

'I thank Heaven for bringing you safely back to the misty shores of hospitable Albion', wrote Bobrowski on 1 May 1881. Conrad was now sent a larger allowance, partly to sponsor further study but also in recognition of his new maturity. This maturity was noticed by Bobrowski in the fluent, lively letters he was receiving and which promped him to

Conrad's 'hired home', 6 Dynevor Road, today. Conrad lived here from 1880 to 1886, between voyages.

Author's Photograph

suggest that Conrad should write travel pieces for the Warsaw press, which 'would bring you some benefit and provide you with a pleasant recreation, while giving pleasure to others'. Conrad wrote nothing for the Warsaw press. It is tempting to think, however, that his uncle's words helped to stimulate an emerging realisation that real-life adventure might be turned into powerful fiction.

It was, in fact, very soon after his uncle's encouraging words that Conrad dreamed up his first sea-going yarn. This, however, was designed to deceive rather than to entertain. He wrote Bobrowski a 'desperate letter' about a shipwreck in which he had been involved. Deeply shocked, Bobrowski sent money to replace lost belongings. Conrad had achieved his objective. There had never been a shipwreck, but he was now £10 better off. Only a few days later Conrad - maintaining his story - promised to pay the money back, clearly feeling guilty at the distress he had caused. Fate should not have been tempted with such a tale. His next ship, the *Palestine*, would provide him with more danger than even his fertile imagination could conjure.

'A regular dose of the east'

'O Youth! The strength of it, the faith of it, the imagination of it! To me she was not an old rattle trap carting about the world a lot of coal for a freight - to me she was the endeavour, the test, the trial of life. I think of her with pleasure , with affection, with regret - as you would think of someone dead you have loved.'

So Charley Marlow speaks of his ship *Judea* in *Youth*, a tale which draws upon Conrad's dramatic experiences on the *Palestine*. Conrad's first voyage to the east was a significant event, but on joining her as second mate he was not quite as disposed to overlook the shortcomings of his ship as his fictional counterpart. In a letter of 11 September, Bobrowski chided his nephew's pompous attitudes towards the mere 'barque' upon which he was to sail, to the £4 a month he was to earn and to his 'creature' of a captain. In fact, Conrad had good reason to complain. The ship was barely seaworthy as she put out from Newcastle on 29 November, bound for Bangkok with a cargo of coal. When she reached the English Channel and was buffeted by a series of heavy gales, her moribund condition resulted in the loss of sails and the springing of a serious leak. The crew of thirteen, Conrad included, refused to proceed on their voyage and put into Falmouth. His letter about this to his uncle elicited a concerned response:

> *'I have never considered that I had the right to order you about, especially now that you are 24 years old, but all the same I sincerely advise you not to go to sea in such a lamentable ship as yours. Danger is certainly part of a sailor's life, but the profession itself should not prevent you from having a sensible attachment to life nor from taking sensible steps to preserve it. Both your Captain Beard and you appear to me like desperate men who look for knocks and wounds, while your ship-owner is a rascal who risks the lives of 10 good men for the sake of a blackguardly profit.'*

The 'carcass of a ship' was delayed for many months in Falmouth, each repair seeming to keep even less water out. In *Youth*, Charley Marlow relates the oppressive feeling of frustration Conrad himself must have felt:

> *'It was horrid. Morally it was worse than pumping for life. It seemed as though we had been forgotten by the world, belonged to nobody, would get nowhere; it seemed that, as if bewitched, we would have to live for ever and ever in that inner harbour, a derision and a by word to generations of long-shore loafers and dishonest boatmen.'*

Marlow's attempts to alleviate such dispiriting boredom might very well have been those chosen by Conrad. With three months' pay in hand, he made an expensive rush for London: 'I went to a music-hall ... lunched, dined, and supped in a swell place in Regent Street, and was back to time, with nothing but a complete set of Byron's works and a new railway rug to show for three months' work.' Whether Conrad perused Byron or not, he later brought to mind a five-shilling edition of Shakespeare 'read in Falmouth at odd moments of the day, to the noisy accompaniment of Caulkers' mallets'. Eventually, on 17 September 1882, the ship put out again, properly repaired, for Bangkok. This time, despite the difficulty of sailing in high winds, it seemed as though they would finally reach their destination unhampered.

The disaster began insidiously. On 11 March the men noticed an ominous smell of burning. The following day smoke was detected from the cargo hold. The men realised with horror that the coal was slowly burning. Attempts were made to douse the affected area and boats were lowered into the water. By the 13th the crisis required increasingly desperate remedies. Four tons of coal were thrown overboard and more water was poured into the hold. But even these measures failed to quell the pent-up energy of the fire. Marlow's description of the inevitable explosion again echoes Conrad's own traumatic experience:

> 'The coal-dust suspended in the air of the hold had glowed dull-red at the moment of the explosion ... It was quick like a rebound. The deck was a wilderness of smashed timber, lying cross wise like trees in a wood after a hurricane; an immense curtain of solid rags waved gently before me - it was the mainsail blown to strips ... I did not know that I had no hair, no eyebrows, no eyelashes, that my young moustache was burnt off, that my face was black, one cheek laid open, my nose cut, and my chin bleeding.'

Once Conrad and the crew had recovered their senses, provisions were put into the life boats and an emergency bearing made for the Sumatra shore. Distress signals were made to another ship, the *S.S. Somerset*, which took the stricken *Palestine* in tow. Fanned by the breeze, the fire erupted dramatically skyward. The *Somerset* slipped her ropes and all hands abandoned ship with, according to the official report, 'the mate and 4 seamen in one boat, the 2nd mate with three hands in another and the master in the long boat with 3 men'. The life boats drifted around the ship as 'she burned furiously; mournful and imposing like a funeral pile kindled in the night, surrounded by the sea, watched over by the stars'. Early in the morning of the 15th the *Palestine* 'went down, head first, in a great hiss of steam' and Conrad piloted his first modest command towards the 'mysterious East ... perfumed like a flower, silent like death, dark like a grave.'

He arrived at Muntock, an island off the coast of Sumatra, thirteen hours later - quite long enough in small boats, if not the many days described in *Youth*. His first experience of the East was a momentous affair, never to be forgotten. He looked back upon the awe-inspiring occasion through Marlow's eyes:

'I see it now - the wide sweep of the bay, the glittering sands, the wealth of green infinite and varied, the sea blue like the sea of a dream, the crowd of attentive faces, the blaze of vivid colour - the water reflecting it all ... I have known its fascination since; I have seen the mysterious shores, the still water, the lands of brown nations, where a stealthy Nemesis lies in wait, pursues, overtakes so many of the conquering race, who are proud of their wisdom, of their knowledge, of their strength. But for me all the East is contained in that vision of my youth. It is all in that moment when I opened my young eyes on it. I came upon it from a tussle with the sea - and I was young - and I saw it looking at me.'

Singapore Harbour

British Library

On 2 April the Marine Court of Enquiry was held in Singapore to investigate the loss of the *Palestine*. It concluded that 'the vessel was not prematurely abandoned and that no blame is attached to the master, officers, or crew.' As second mate, Conrad would no doubt have been questioned on these matters. The eponymous hero of *Lord Jim* would later undergo just such an experience:

> *'The face of the presiding magistrate, clean shaved and impassible, looked at him deadly pale between the red faces of the two nautical assessors. The light of a broad window under the ceiling fell from above on the heads and shoulders of the three men, and they were fiercely distinct in the half-light of the big court room where the audience seemed composed of staring shadows. They wanted facts. Facts!'*

Conrad wrote to his uncle shortly after the hearing, presumably recounting the most recent adventures of 'the year in which I came nearest to death at sea, first by water and then by fire'. They both agreed that, after some five years, it was time they met again. Marienbad in Czechoslovakia was the planned rendez-vous, where Bobrowski intended to take the waters for stomach problems and mud baths for his rheumatism. He assured his nephew that 'this month spent together will be a rest for you, a cure for me, and a long awaited pleasure for us both'. Conrad left London in July 1883. Although he arrived without the first mate's certificate and British citizenship eagerly hoped for by his uncle, both were overjoyed to be reunited and spent pleasant days in Marienbad and Toeplitz. Seeing his uncle again filled Conrad with memories of his family, and of those who had cared for him when he was younger. In one of his earliest surviving letters, to Stefan Buszczynski, Conrad enclosed a rather puzzled-looking photograph of himself and pondered his place in the world:

A photograph of Conrad sent from Marienbad in 1883.

British Library

'I am leaving here for London in a few days; from there I do not know where fate will take me. During the last few years - that is since my first examination, I have not been too happy in my journeyings. I was nearly drowned, nearly got burned, but generally my health is good, I am not short of courage or of the will to work or of love for my profession; and I always remember what you said when I was leaving Cracow: "Remember" - you said - "wherever you may sail you are sailing towards Poland". That I have never forgotten, and never will forget.'

Conrad headed back to his rooms in Stoke Newington, his apprehension of the future sharpened after the carefree days spent with Bobrowski. An emotional letter sent from the younger man soon after they parted apparently contained words which its recipient thought worth keeping 'sealed up in my heart'. Conrad's letter (lost in the Russian revolution of 1917, like all of those to his uncle) must have spoken of their mutual loneliness. Bobrowski confessed to him in his reply that 'you were right in supposing that on returning to Toeplitz I was sad and melancholy, sitting down alone to my evening cup of tea, opposite the empty chair of my Admiral!!!' Conrad also received a reply from Buszczynski, who marvelled at 'the many sad and terrifying adventures that befell you on your journeys' and thanked him for the portrait he had sent, which 'touched me deeply'.

On 10 September 1883, Conrad joined the *Riversdale*, a fifteen-hundred-ton sailing ship, as second mate. On reaching Madras he left the ship, having fallen out with his captain, L. B. McDonald. On his certificate of discharge, dated 17 April 1884, McDonald found himself unable to comment on his officer's 'character and conduct'. A letter of 8 December 1884, sent to Conrad after his return to London from Bobrowski's brother Kazimierz, congratulated him on 'winning the case against your ex-captain'. Whatever the matter had been, it appears serious enough to have reached the courts.

Conrad returned to London as second mate on the *Narcissus*, a voyage later given an extraordinarily powerful treatment in *The Nigger of the Narcissus*. The violently stormy conditions around the Cape of Good Hope described in the tale are those which he himself endured:

Crew list of the Narcissus.

National Maritime Museum

'Tremendous dull blows made the ship tremble while she rolled under the weight of the seas toppling on her deck. At times she soared up swiftly as if to to leave this earth for ever, then during interminable moments fell through a void with all the hearts on board of her standing still, till a frightful shock, expected and sudden, started them off again with a big thump ... Now and then, for the fraction of an intolerable second, the ship, in the fiercer burst of a terrible uproar, remained on her side, vibrating and still, with a stillness more appalling than the wildest motion.'

Conrad arrived in Dunkirk on the 16 October. Once in London, he applied himself to his studies and took his examination for first mate. He failed his initial attempt, on 17 November, but on 3 December 'escaped the room thankfully - passed!'. He joined his next ship, the *Tilkhurst*, as second mate, the following April. She was registered at Hull and bound for the East. The sailing ship put in at Cardiff before its long journey to Singapore. In Cardiff, Conrad undertook a favour on behalf of a Polish sailor he had met. He was to repay a small loan to another compatriot. When he arrived, he immediately became friends with the creditor's son, Spiridion Kliszczewski.

Conrad had a fine passage to Singapore, arriving in September. He took the opportunity to strike up a correspondence with his new friend, writing his earliest surviving letters in the English language (complete with frequent infelicities of expression and errors of spelling). The young men's discussions of English politics were thrown into relief by a haunting awareness of their own country's tragic history. The exchanges prompted Conrad to consider the whole question of belonging and allegiance:

'I agree with you that in a free and hospitable land even the most persecuted of our race may find relative peace and a certain amount of happiness - materially at least; consequently I understood and readily accepted your reference to "home." When speaking, writing or thinking in English the word Home always means for me the hospitable shores of Great Britain.'

It was during this time that the man hitherto known as Korzeniowski decided to start signing himself by the less obviously foreign name of Conrad.

'Material happiness' was indeed something else Conrad pondered, whilst on the other side of the globe. The ship had by now sailed on to Calcutta and from here the second mate spelled out his latest plans: 'I wish to start due North! - In other words and speaking - (as everybody ought) plainly my soul is bent upon a whaling adventure.' Conrad had done his research, claiming to be 'brimfull with the most exhaustive information upon the subject', having 'read, studied, pumped professional men and imbibed knowledge upon whale fishing and sealing for the last four years.' These plans came to nothing; even their author suspected they might be the 'ravings of an unbusinesslike lunatic'.

Although his 'ravings' might have seemed yet one more sign of restlessness, Conrad's wishes probably sprang from an ultimate desire for more not less stability. His captain thought him excellent but he increasingly wished to be his own master. Bobrowski wanted this too and kept up the pressure on him to take his final exam and to secure naturalisation as a British citizen: 'I shall cease to make a nuisance of myself once you have settled these two affairs.'

There were other reasons behind Conrad's desire for a new start in the fresh blankness of the north. The 'stealthy Nemesis of the East' was becoming too much for him. Just before the torrid voyage to Calcutta two members of the crew had an ugly fight. The severe head injury sustained by one of them, William Cumming, resulted in a delirium followed by a suicidal jump overboard. On his previous voyage one of the crew, Joseph Barron, had died slowly of fever. Both episodes haunted him as they went on to haunt his novel, *The Nigger of the Narcissus*.

It was a 'bad passage' of 158 days before the *Tilkhurst* arrived at Dundee on 16 June 1886 with its

The Tilkhurst

National Maritime Museum

cargo of jute. Conrad made for London with just enough experience to qualify him for entrance to the master's exam. On 11 November, having failed once in July, he went again into the examination room. He had been able to call himself a British subject since 19 August; now, emerging onto Tower Hill, he could also call himself a British master mariner:

> 'That fact, satisfactory and obscure in itself, had for me a certain ideal significance. It was an answer to certain outspoken scepticism, and even to some not very kind aspersions. I had vindicated myself from what had been cried upon as a stupid obstinacy or a fantastic caprice.'

Yet during the very period of his triumph, Conrad was busy laying the foundations of his next career. By the end of 1886, a period spent in London without a berth, he had apparently completed his earliest surviving work of fiction, a short story, 'The Black Mate'.

'Long live the "Ordin, Master in the British Merchant Service"!! May he live long! May he be healthy and may every success attend him in every enterprise both on sea and on land!'. Bobrowski was delighted that Conrad had vindicated himself, and it was now as first mate that his nephew signed on for the *Highland Forest* on 16 February 1887 in Amsterdam for a wage of £7 a month. Despite the hopeless conditions, the ship frozen in like the many other 'corpses of vessels in a white world', he was a proud man: 'I think that in those days I never forgot the fact of my elevation for five consecutive minutes. I fancy it kept me warm, even in my slumbers, better than the high pile of blankets, which positively crackled with frost as I threw them off in the morning.'

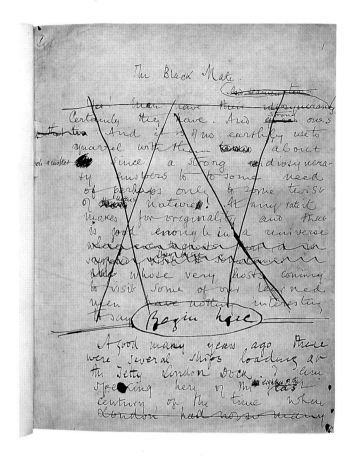

'The Black Mate': the first manuscript page of Conrad's earliest surviving work of fiction.

British Library
Ashley MS 2949, f.1

Conrad's pride took a fall shortly after they had set sail for Samarang in Java. Before the captain arrived, he had organised the loading of the ship but in such a way that he had made her 'cranky'. 'Neither before nor since have I felt a ship roll so abruptly, so violently, so heavily', recalled an older and wiser Conrad. The captain left it to the sea to teach his junior a lesson. As the ship began to strain under the pressure, a 'piece of one of the minor spars ... flew against the chief mate's back, and sent him sliding on his face for quite a considerable distance along the main deck.' Conrad too suffered an injury, symptomized, as he recalled, by 'inexplicable periods of powerlessness' and 'sudden accesses of mysterious pain'. This resulted in a spell in a 'great airy ward' of a Singapore hospital - and a good deal of suspicion on the part of his uncle. Bobrowski was mindful of the strange nervous afflictions which Conrad had suffered as a child and of the nearly fatal consequences of his depression in Marseilles. The problems Conrad reported with his leg aroused his suspicions:

'You did not write to me exactly what the trouble is; is it ordinary rheumatism? or sciatica? - or perhaps paralysis? It could be any of these. I am racking my brains to think what it can be!? I would like to think it is something slight, but the sad experience I have gone through with persons dear to me continually eggs me on to think the worst.'

By 22 August 1887, after some weeks spent in hospital, Conrad was well enough to join a small coastal steamer, the *Vidar*, as first mate. His impressions, as he cruised for nineteen weeks around the ports on the shores of Celebes and Borneo, ferrying 'wandering traders of good repute', would later provide characters and atmosphere for his early novels and short stories. It was while sailing up the Berau River in Borneo that he met the man who would inspire the tragically absurd hero of his first novel, *Almayer's Folly*. Charles William Olmeijer was a European-Asian Dutchman living in the small settlement Tandjong Redeb, closed in by 'immense and gloomy forests'. The man's reputation as a dreamer whose fantastic projections were perpetually undercut by the pathetic realities of his lonely situation fascinated Conrad (one of whose tasks on the voyage was to deliver to him a donkey, an animal hopelessly unsuited to the environment). Although 'he governed his conduct by considerations removed from the obvious, by incredible assumptions, which rendered his logic impenetrable to any reasonable person,' Conrad perhaps saw in Olmeijer something of his own youthful and dogged romanticism. At any rate, he would one day acknowledge a great debt to the man. 'If I had not got to know Almayer pretty well', he wrote, 'it is almost certain there would never have been a line of mine in print.'

Conrad resigned his position on the 5 January 1888. Although apparently suffering from a liver complaint, two weeks later he signed on in Singapore for the iron barque *Otago*. At thirty years of age he was finally a captain, 'which', he later informed a fellow Pole, 'was not bad for a foreigner without influence'. Conrad joined the ship at Bangkok on 24 January, sailing on 9 February for Australia with a cargo of teak. His experiences were intially, at least, as gloomy as those upon the *Narcissus* and the *Tilkhurst*. On the first part of the voyage all the crew, save the cook, fell seriously ill with fever. On her arrival at Singapore, the ship was put outside harbour limits and Conrad sought medical help for his men. Six new crew members joined the ship as she set sail for Sydney. The first mate was Charles Born, remembered with some dislike by his captain:

> *'He had an extremely disturbing air of being everlastingly ready (even when seated at table at my right hand before a plate of salt beef) to grapple with some impending calamity ... His eternally watchful demeanour, his jerky, nervous talk, even his, as it were, determined silences, seemed to imply - and, I believe, they did imply - that to his mind the ship was never safe in my hands.'*

When the ship arrived, safely enough, in early May, Conrad found letters written by his uncle. One of them was a simple list of the possessions which had been gathering dust since his parents had left Warsaw twenty-eight years earlier: a set of silver cutlery for twelve people, two silver-plated trays, an antique clock, an arm-chair, a small table, table linen and 'various knick-knacks, neither beautiful nor valuable, deposited in a separate chest'. This laconic report of Conrad's pitiful inheritance must have made him feel sad and strange on the other side of the globe. He had not much to show for his thirty years.

Towards the end of his life, Conrad remembered the moment when 'all of a sudden, all the deep-lying historic sense of the exploring adventures in the Pacific surged up to the surface of my being'. He wrote to the owners of the *Otago* 'suggesting that, instead of the usual southern route, I should take the ship to Mauritius by way of Torres Strait'. Conrad wished to sail the romantic course he had read about as a child, the course which the early navigators had taken. As a young boy Conrad had escaped the privations and miseries of his unpredictable life through tales of the sea; as an adolescent, he abandoned those tales for tough reality; as a man he had achieved the highest rank of his profession. Now, by a curious return to the texts of his early years, he was becoming increasingly aware of the imaginative possibilities of his own experiences.

To Conrad's amazement, his paymasters agreed to humour him. To the equal astonishment of the pilot and tug-master, the *Otago* left Sydney in a heavy gale to avoid the calms. The Strait was soon reached: 'It was not without a certain emotion that, commanding very likely the first, and certainly the last, merchant ship that carried a cargo that way - from Sydney to Mauritius - I put her head at daybreak for Bligh's Entrance, and packed on her every bit of canvas she could carry.' Conrad's voyage was a profoundly affecting experience. He passed two wrecks, one of which 'loomed up, a sinister and enormous *memento mori* raised ... above the far-away line of the horizon drawn under the sinking sun' and passed close to the 'insignificant crumb of dark earth' upon which Captain Cook had landed from the *Endeavour*. According to Gérard Jean-Aubry, one of Conrad's earliest biographers, one of the charterers of the *Otago*, Paul Langlois, remembered many years later the impressive and enigmatic figure who brought the boat into Port Louis, Mauritius, after this extraordinary voyage:

> *'He had vigorous, extremely mobile features which would change very quickly from gentleness to an excitability bordering on anger; large black eyes which were as a rule melancholy and dreamy, and gentle, too, except in his quite frequent moments of irritation; a determined chin, a well-shaped handsome mouth, and a thick, well-trimmed dark brown moustache - such was his appearance, certainly agreeable but, above all, strange in its expression and difficult to forget...'*

Conrad dressed extravagantly, wearing 'fancy' trousers and carrying a gold-topped cane. But despite his 'varied and interesting fund of conversation', he was frequently 'taciturn and irritable'. Langlois recalled that 'on such days he would have a nervous tic in the shoulder and eyes: anything unexpected, something falling on the floor or the slam of a door, would make him jump'. In Conrad's day such symptoms would be referred to simply as a 'nerves'. Today's psychiatrist might read them more as signs of acute anxiety.

Langlois goes on to draw a picture of a reclusive and mysterious man. His frequent absence from the company of other sailors might, however, be explained by the fact that Conrad was spending much of his time with the well established Renouf family. He had met one of the younger seafaring members of the family in Bombay and now renewed the acquaintance. The man in question, Gabriel, introduced him to his attractive sisters, with whom he flirted and apparently played a game of confidences - the written results of which are presented by his biographer Jean-Aubry. Among the confessions, Conrad described his principal characteristic as laziness, named Lapland as the country in which he would best like to live (still evidently interested in the North), claimed he preferred both blondes and brunettes and that more than anything else, like Marlow in *Heart of Darkness*, he hated false pretences.

During the eight weeks of his stay in the port, Conrad apparently fell in love with one of his 'confessors', the twenty-six-year-old Eugenie. Two days before departing for Melbourne he asked her brother for her hand in marriage. On discovering that she was already betrothed, he retired to the *Otago*, decreeing never again to set foot on the island. Although several commentators accept that Jean-Aubry's account of the Port Louis episode needs to be treated with caution, it would be unwise to discount it altogether.

On 26 March 1889, Conrad resigned his command of the *Otago*. The owners of the ship pointed out in a letter of 2 April that 'this early severance from our employ is entirely at your own desire, with a view to visiting Europe, and that we entertain a high opinion of your ability in the capacity you now vacate, of your attainments generally, and should be glad to learn of your future success'. Conrad may have resigned his command to avoid returning from Australia to Mauritius and its unhappy associations. But perhaps, after fourteen months with the ship, he simply craved a return to the west: as Marlow phrased it in *Heart of Darkness* he had, after all, endured 'a regular dose of the East'.

The Otago

National Maritime Museum

〜 'Into the heart of an immense darkness'

Opposite:

Bessborough Gardens today. Conrad started writing Almayer's Folly *here.*

Author's Photograph

Conrad arrived back in London in June 1889 after sailing from Australia as a passenger. He had been away from the city for twenty-eight months. He found rented accommodation in Bessborough Gardens, Pimlico, and made half-hearted efforts to find another ship: 'My whole being was steeped in the indolence of a sailor away from the sea, the scene of never-ending labour and of unceasing duty.' His friends Krieger and Hope, together with Bobrowski, had helped him to establish a small financial interest in a company of shipping agents called Barr, Moering and Co. In the middle of a bustling part of the city full of shipping offices and societies, this served as a convenient base from which he could toy with the idea of obtaining another berth. From here he turned down an offer to sail to Mexico and the West Indies.

Conrad's preoccupation was not so much with the future as with recent history. Olmeijer in particular came to haunt him in his lodgings close to the Thames which, with its 'opaline mist', seemed to merge into its Eastern counterpart, the Berau. Despite his urban surroundings, Conrad saw in his mind's eye the sad Dutchman 'moving across a patch of burnt grass, a blurred, shadowy shape'. His entourage, too, 'came with silent and irresistible appeal'. Conrad felt compelled to take up his pen, inescapably attended in this way by events and characters from his past, who 'began to live again with a vividness and poignancy'. He later evoked the character of the day which he came to regard as the first of his writing life:

> 'It was an autumn day with an opaline atmosphere, a veiled, semi-opaque, lustrous day, with fiery points and flashes of red sunlight on the roofs and windows opposite, while the trees of the square with all their leaves gone were like tracings of indian ink on a sheet of tissue paper. It was one of those London days that have the charm of mysterious amenity, of fascinating softness.'

Conrad's first novel, *Almayer's Folly* was certainly not conceived as a money-making enterprise. Its author claimed that 'there was no vision of a printed book before me as I sat writing' and its tortuous progress delayed him from earning much-needed income. Conrad's attempts to obtain another position became more earnest. The job he eventually found would expose him, in the space of just one year, to places, people and experiences destined to shake him to the very core of his being. It would also provide, some ten years further on, the inspiration for one of the world's most profoundly unsettling literary masterpieces, *Heart of Darkness*.

In November, Conrad went to see Albert Thys, director of the Societé Belge du Haut-Congo in Brussels, hoping to secure a position with the company's African operations. Brussels itself seemed foreboding and sinister; he recalled a 'narrow and deserted street in deep shadow, high houses, innumerable windows with venetian blinds, a dead silence, grass sprouting between the stones, immense double doors standing ponderously ajar.' In his childhood, Africa had seemed to Conrad full of mystery. The great empty spaces in maps of the continent - almost as blank as the oceans - allowed him to dream up fantastic adventures: 'Regions unknown! My imagination could depict to itself there worthy, adventurous and devoted men, nibbling at the edges ... conquering a bit of truth here and a bit of truth there.' Such naive wonder had not deserted the man approaching his thirty-second birthday. Conrad agreed with Thys to serve for three years as a river steamboat officer in the Belgian Congo.

'Odd thing that I, who used to to clear out for any part of the world at twenty-four hours' notice, with less thought than most men give to the crossing of a street, had a moment - I won't say of hesitation, but of startled pause, before this commonplace affair.' The words are Marlow's, the narrator and protagonist of *Heart of Darkness*, but almost certainly record Conrad's own trepidation. He had only a spoken agreement with Thys at this stage and no definite commitment to any particular steamer. His sense of foreboding nevertheless prompted him to make plans to visit Bobrowski in Poland. In addition to the uncertainties surrounding his own future, his uncle's health had further declined and Conrad wished to take the opportunity to see him - possibly for the last time.

Conrad arranged to travel to his uncle via Brussels, where he planned to call briefly on a distant cousin, Aleksander Poradowski, and his wife Marguerite, a beautiful and intelligent novelist, journalist and short-story writer. Conrad arrived on 5 February to find Aleksander gravely ill. When he reached Warsaw on the next leg of his journey he discovered that his relative had died and wrote to console Marguerite: 'I was with you in thought and spirit yesterday, sharing, though far from you, your sorrow, as indeed I have not stopped doing since I left you.' In the short time they spent together, the pair had established a close relationship which would develop further in correspondence. Conrad could see in Marguerite many of the things he wished to be: urbane, accomplished, admired and influential. In his next letter he revealed that he had described her to others as 'I have known you, kind, loving, devoted and spirited'. Carrying with him the manuscript of *Almayer's Folly* 'as if it were a talisman or a treasure' he told her that he had already finished reading hers, 'Yaga' - twice.

The last leg of his journey to Bobrowski was made by sled, Conrad dressed in 'an enormous bear-skin travelling coat' and having a 'delightful boyish feeling of coming home from school'.

Marguerite Poradowski, Conrad's beautiful and influential 'aunt'.

Duke University

'*I saw again the sun setting on the plains as I saw it in the travels of my childhood. It set, clear and red, dipping into the snow in full view as if it were setting on the sea. It was twenty-three years since I had seen the sun set over that land; and we drove on in the darkness which fell swiftly upon the livid expanse of snows till, out of the waste of a white earth joining a bestarred sky, surged up black shapes, the clumps of trees about a village of the Ukrainian plain. A cottage or two glided by, a low, interminable wall and then, glimmering and twinkling through a screen of fir trees, the lights of the master's house.'*

On 4 February, Conrad was reunited with the sixty-one-year-old who 'had been for a quarter of a century the wisest, firmest, the most indulgent of guardians, extending over me a paternal care and affection, a moral support which I seemed to feel always near me in the most distant parts of the earth.' Bobrowski had not slept for four days, excited at the prospect of seeing his 'wandering nephew' again. When he arrived, he handed to him a document begun in 1869 giving a full account of what 'the making of a man out of Mr. Konrad had cost'. The act revealed at once the extraordinary care he had taken to support Conrad and the faith he now felt in his independence and 'maturity'.

In between trips into the countryside, Conrad continued with the manuscript of *Almayer's Folly*, which grew 'line by line, rather than page by page'. He fretted about the lack of news from Thys and complained to Marguerite that he felt little hope of his African plans coming to fruition. Almost immediately he received a summons from the company, his 'Aunt' (as he was given to calling her), having intervened on his behalf. He thanked her personally on his journey back to London and by 2 May was preparing for what he hoped would be a three-year stay in Central Africa. The inauspicious death of one of the company's steamer captains had provided an opening for the thirty-three-year-old Conrad. His twenty-nine-year-old predecessor, Johannes Freiesleben, had been killed in a dispute about firewood or fresh provisions.

Conrad sent his relatives photographs and packed his precious manuscript which jostled for space with 'tin boxes ... revolvers ... high boots'. At Bordeaux he joined the ship upon which he was to make the first stage of his journey, the *Ville de Maceio*. Tenerife was the first port of call and from here he shared his dark and uneasy mood with Marguerite:

'We left Bordeaux on a rainy day. Dismal day, a not very cheerful departure,
some haunting memories, some vague regrets, some still vaguer hopes. One
doubts the future. For indeed - I ask myself - why should anyone believe in it?
A little illusion, many dreams, a rare flash of happiness followed by
disillusionment, a little anger and much suffering, and then the end.'

Conrad also wrote to Bobrowski, who responded with the hope that his nephew had
'not already been cooked on a spit and eaten as a roast'. He continued in a tone
which made clear to Conrad that he had little time for the motives of Europeans in
Africa:

'You are probably looking around at people and things as well as the 'civilizing'
(confound it) affair in the machinery of which you are a cog - before you feel
able to acquire and express your own opinion. Don't wait however until it all
crystallizes into clear sentences, but tell me something of your health and your
first impressions.'

These particular words stuck in Conrad's mind. One of the major themes of
Heart of Darkness concerns the strain language suffers in its attempt to clearly
articulate evil - more particularly the evil of white 'civilized' men in Africa.

The ship reached Boma, just above the Congo estuary, on 12 June. The next
day Conrad sailed on a small steamer up river to Matadi. First he sent his aunt
another letter:

'No new events. As to feelings, also nothing new, and there is the trouble. For,
if one could unburden oneself of one's heart, one's memory (and also - one's brain)
and obtain a whole new set of these things, life would become perfectly diverting.
As this is impossible, life is not perfectly diverting. It is abominably sad!'

Conrad suggests that he would like to exchange his tedious life for one far
more exciting. That he should write this at this precise stage, fully aware that only

seven per cent of company employees managed to fulfil their three-year contract, suggests a good deal of nervous bravura.

From the moment he started his long trek overland from Matadi to Kinshasa he might well have wished for another life. Not, however, as a result of tedium. At Matadi he started a diary. The entries, although laconic, speak volumes. With the exception of the future Irish patriot, Roger Casement, with whom he established a friendship, he found the greedy and argumentative Europeans around him repugnant.

Matadi in February 1890.

British Library

His diary records an intention to 'avoid acquaintances as much as possible'. As he penetrated deeper into the country the irritation of squabbling traders seemed nothing compared to new and terrible scenes. On 3 July he came across a body so badly decomposed he was not able to work out whether or not the poor victim of this ingnominious death had been shot. The next day he 'saw another dead body lying by the path in an attitude of meditative repose'. By 5 July he was 'getting jolly well sick of this fun', yet had no choice but to press on. On the 29th he 'passed a skeleton tied up to a post. Also white man's grave - no name.' The last entry, on 1 August, records a further litany of horrors together with Conrad's attempts to act kindly in the face of an appalling general indifference to human suffering:

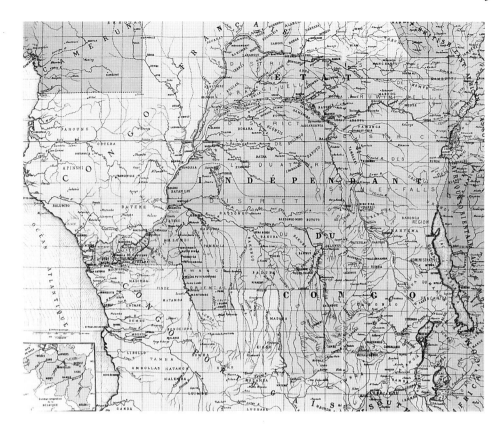

A map of the Congo, contemporary with Conrad's expedition.

British Library

A group of carriers, around the time of Conrad's expedition.

British Library

'*Row between the carriers and a man stating himself in Government employ, about a mat. Blows with sticks raining hard. Stopped it. Chief came with a youth about 13 suffering from gunshot wound in the head. Bullet entered about an inch above the right eyebrow and came out a little inside...Gave him a little glycerine...Glad to see the end of this stupid tramp.*'

Conrad reached the Company's next base, at Kinshasa, on 2 August. Here he joined the steamer the *Roi des Belges*. Conrad was not given command, a role filled by a Dane, Ludvig Koch. He was allocated instead the task of making a meticulous navigational record of the journey - something which must have wounded the pride of a British master mariner fresh from commanding ships on the open seas. Bobrowski certainly noted 'a deep resentment towards the Belgians for exploiting you so mercilessly'.

Camille Delcommune, described in Heart of Darkness *as a 'papier-mâché Mephistopheles'.*

British Library

The rickety 'tin-pot steamer' arrived at Stanley Falls, 'the farthest point of navigation', on 1 September, having made the 1000 mile journey remarkably quickly. Conrad had finally fulfilled his 'boyish boast' to adventure into the heart of Africa. Yet in the last year of his life he recalled emotions of bitter disappointment:

'*A great melancholy descended on me. Yes, this was the very spot. But there was no shadowy friend to stand by my side in the night of enormous wilderness, no great haunting memory, but only the ... distasteful knowledge of the vilest scramble for loot that ever disfigured the history of human conscience and geographical exploration. What an end to the idealised realities of a boy's daydreams!*'

After several days in this lonely, degraded place of shattered dreams, Conrad was asked by the company's most senior representative in Africa, Camille Delcommune, to take over command of the *Roi des Belges*.

Above:

Le Roi des Belges, *Conrad's 'tin pot steamer'.*

A group of Africans visit Le Roi des Belges. *In* Heart of Darkness *such a visit becomes an attack.*

Koch was ill with fever, as was the station's agent, George Antoine Klein. The steamer made swift progress downstream. Klein (one possible source for Conrad's terrifyingly malign Mr Kurtz in *Heart of Darkness*), died on 21 September and was hastily buried in the jungle. By the time the steamer had reached Kinshasa three days later, Koch had resumed command.

Conrad felt increasingly dejected. He wrote to his cousin Maria Tyszkowa that 'I have lived long enough to realize that life is full of griefs and sorrows which no one can escape'. The picture became blacker still when he found out that his plans to obtain a better position with another expedition had been scuppered by Delcommune, for whom he was developing a considerable hatred. The man, two years younger than Conrad, had been a constant presence and irritation since 3 August. All Conrad's simmering resentment poured out in a long letter to Marguerite of 26 September:

Camille Delcommune's brother, Alexandre (left), who becomes leader of the 'Eldorado Exploring Expedition' in Heart of Darkness.

British Library

'Everything here is repellent to me. Men and things, but men above all. And I am repellent to them also. From the manager in Africa who has taken the trouble to tell one and all that I offend him supremely, down to the lowest mechanic, they all have the gift of irritating my nerves ... The manager is a common ivory dealer with base instincts who considers himself a merchant although he is only a kind of African shop-keeper.'

Conrad revealed that his health had been far from good. He had suffered from fever and dysentry and felt 'weak physically and not a little demoralized'. He missed the open sea 'which has so often lulled me' and regretted deeply 'having tied myself down for three years'. In fact, his illness soon became so severe that he was released from his obligations to the company. The letter he wrote on 19 October worried Bobrowski not so much because of its gloomy contents but because of its actual appearance: 'I found your handwriting so changed - which I ascribe to the weakening and exhausting effect of fever and dysentry.' Little is known of Conrad in the last two months of 1890, other than that his health was extremely precarious.

Conrad re-emerged in Brussels towards the end of January. Some of his feelings of utter despondency and misanthropy are given voice by Marlow in *Heart of Darkness*:

'No, they did not bury me, though there is a period of time which I remember mistily, with a shuddering wonder, like a passage through some inconceivable world that had no hope in it and no desire. I found myself back in the sepulchral city resenting the sight of people hurrying through the streets to filch a little money from each other, to devour their infamous cookery, to gulp their unwholesome beer, to dream their insignificant and silly dreams. They trespassed upon my thoughts ... they could not possibly know the things I knew.'

By the 1 February he was back in London, his hair thinner, and one of his legs badly swollen. 'I could hardly wait to run to the doctor', he wrote to Marguerite. A week later he told her that 'I feel myself stronger and more disposed to live'. The statement should not be regarded as flippant; years later he

remembered that 'before the departure of the steamer which was to take me home I had the time to wish myself dead over and over again with perfect sincerity'.

Conrad's time in the Congo would affect him physically and spiritually for the rest of his life. The seven months he spent there awoke in him a terrible insight into the folly and pathos of human behaviour and motivation. In Marlow's words: 'It was the farthest point of navigation and the culminating point of my experience. It seemed somehow to throw a kind of light on everything about me - and into my thoughts. It was sombre enough, too - and pitiful.' Edward Garnett, a friend whose great importance to Conrad will be seen later, felt certain that the 'sinister voice of the Congo with its murmuring undertone of human fatuity, baseness and greed, had swept away the generous illusions of his youth and had left him gazing into the heart of an immense darkness'.

And from the very beginning, the nightmare was difficult to escape. When he arrived back in London it was to a press filled with appalling accounts of the behaviour of members of H. M. Stanley's expedition to rescue Emin Pasha. Two years before Conrad ventured up the Congo one of the party, an eminently erudite and civilized man by the name of James Sligo Jameson, had reputedly allowed the wilderness to get the better of him. Pursuing his scientific enthusiasms to extremes, he had apparently paid six handkerchiefs for the privilege of watching and sketching a young slave girl sacrificed and eaten by cannibals. This and other aspects of Jameson's behaviour may well have been in Conrad's mind when he came to write *Heart of Darkness* and in particular to create Kurtz, an 'emissary of pity, and science, and progress' whose terrifying decline into savagery caused him, among other things, 'to preside at certain midnight dances ending with unspeakable rites, which ... were offered up to him - do you understand? - to Mr Kurtz himself.'

In no fit state to do so, Conrad bravely tried to put recent events behind him by travelling up to Scotland in search of a command. By the end of February he was back in the German Hospital, Dalston, East London, his loyal friend Krieger probably having arranged for his admission. He told Marguerite that his complaint was rheumatism in the left leg and neuralgia in the right arm, but a letter from his uncle suggests that his mental health required equal attention. Conrad had written a letter from hospital which, Bobrowski responded, 'grieved me deeply and gave me the impression that you are dispirited and weak'. He implored Conrad to co-operate with his doctor 'by not yielding to lassitude or depression'. Such words of encouragement were not enough. The next letter from Conrad was so 'full of sadness and despondency', that his uncle could not bring himself to reveal how upset it had made him. On 1 May, Conrad informed Marguerite that 'my nerves are disordered, which results in palpitations of the heart and attacks of breathlessness'.

Dr Ludvig recommended that Conrad should go to Champel in Switzerland

to receive water treatment, a cure for nervous disorders. 'I am still plunged in densest night, and my dreams are only nightmares', he wrote to Marguerite, a week before leaving England on the 17 May. Once at the Hotel-Pension de la Roseraie, being able to work on the novel must have helped to nurture what little remained of an interest in life: 'At that date there were in existence only seven chapters of "Almayer's Folly, " but the chapter in my history … was that of a long, long illness and very dismal convalescence … Champel is rendered for ever famous by the termination of the eighth chapter in the history of Almayer's decline and fall.'

The stay at Champel improved Conrad's spirits a little, as did frequent yachting trips on the Thames with Hope when he returned to London. Before long, however, Bobrowski detected a still deepening depression and anxiety. In a remarkable letter of 18 July, Conrad asked his uncle to give him a frank account of the shortcomings of his character, observed throughout the thirty-four years of his life. In contrast to the view expressed to Marguerite that 'we are the slaves of Fate even before birth', Conrad was searching deep within for clues to his misery.

Bobrowski wrote back with a sympathetic yet honest reply, remarking that 'I consider that you have always lacked endurance and perserverance in decisions, which is the instability in your aims and desires.' This lack of endurance 'in the face of facts' he thought inherited from the Naleczs, who never seemed to learn that 'the facts most often gave the lie to their dreams'. After Africa, Conrad knew only too well the truth of his uncle's word, which continued:

> *'In your projects you let your imagination run away with you - you become an optimist; but when you encounter disappointments you fall easily into pessimism - and as you have a lot of pride, you suffer more as the result of disappointments than somebody would who had a more moderate imagination but was endowed with greater endurance in activity and relationships.'*

Conrad sought to understand himself by applying to the man who knew him best. But this was not his only approach. *Almayer's Folly*, in common with many of his works, explores precisely this gulf between dreams and facts, imagination and reality. Through his greatest characters Conrad scrutinized within himself the battle between the romantic and the realist. And as he elicits pity in us for their faults, so Bobrowski pitied his: 'These are shortcomings' he wrote, 'but even with them one can be loved.'

Despite this support, Conrad's writing was fitful and his melancholy persisted. Tedious, solitary work managing a warehouse in London for Barr, Moering & Co. hardly helped, despite it being 'undertaken to accustom myself again to the activities of a healthy existence'. Neither did living alone in modest digs at 17 Gillingham Street, near Victoria Station. 'It is better to die young as in any case one is bound to die sometime', he morbidly informed his uncle who decided it was time to address, once and for all, the nature of Conrad's depression. Remembering the crisis in Marseilles, he diagnosed a pessimism caused by a combination of physical weakness and a 'diseased imagination', in which 'one's whole power of resistance has become consumed in dreaming and there is none left for the sober judgement of facts and of the various problems of life, and there is none left for action or counteraction'. He

reminded him that, as Poles, 'we are a collection of proclaimed and generally unrecognized celebrities - whom no one knows, no one acknowledges, and no one ever will!' Therefore, he should leave his unrealistic dreaming aside, together with his scorn for fellow men, and apply himself to a life of tolerance and duty: 'my assertion is: that although this world is not the best that one could imagine, it is nevertheless the only one we know.'

Bobrowski suspected that Conrad's marine career may have contributed to his dreaming, rather than provided a practical antidote to it. It was his return to the open seas, however, which finally helped to lift from him his shroud of depression. 'I have returned quite worn out from my long day at work and feel like going to bed, but ... to you

17 Gillingham Street, Conrad's modest lodgings near Victoria Station.

Author's Photograph

first of all - I must send you the great news.' Thus Conrad informed Marguerite on 14 November 1891 of his berth as first officer aboard the sailing ship *Torrens*, and his departure for Australia in six days' time. 'An active life, even the most commonplace one, is the best remedy for pessimism', wrote his uncle on learning the news; despite his reservations, he was delighted that his nephew would no longer be languishing in London becoming more and more embittered.

Conrad arrived at Port Adelaide on 3 March 1892. An anonymous passenger recalled that he 'was a capital ship's officer, capable and courageous, but inclined to dream a little ... Sailors and boys all swore by him'. On the voyage he had sympathised with an acutely anxious passenger, for whom being at sea seemed a 'sentence of death'. He later commented that 'it was not so long since I had been neurasthenic myself' and had suffered 'a bad breakdown'. Back in Gillingham Street he wrote to Marguerite on 4 September, his outlook now a

Conrad (back row, centre) on board the Torrens, *with apprentices.*

curious fusion of his own bleak pessimism and Bobrowski's considered pragmatism:

> 'one becomes useful only on recognising the extent of the individual's utter insignificance within the arrangement of the universe. When one has fully understood that, by oneself, one is nothing and man is worth neither more nor less than the work he accomplishes with honesty of means and purpose, and within the strict limits of his duty to society, only then is one master of one's conscience, only then has one the right to call oneself a man.'

Conrad embarked for Australia again on 25 October. He arrived 97 days later sombre about an uncertain future - 'or rather', as he put it to Marguerite, 'the certainty of

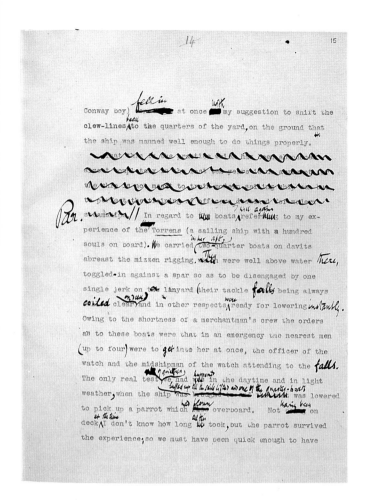

the "uniform grey" awaiting me'. From Cape Town, on the return voyage, he wrote again to congratulate her on her literary successes and to consider his own situation:

'Your life is broadening. Your horizons are enlarging with all the possibilities of a great agglomeration of humanity whose monotonous variety is measured by infinity; my view is circumscribed by the sombre circle where the blue of the sea and the blue of the sky touch without merging. Moving within this perfect circle inscribed by the hand of the Creator, a circle of which I am always the centre, I keep my eyes on the undulating swell, the only movement of which I am certain, and I think of you who live in the tumult of the spirit, where the storms are blown to fury by the inspiration of ideas.'

Conrad's 'sombre circle' of physical and intellectual isolation was about to be temporarily relieved. The manuscript of *Almayer's Folly* had by now 'acquired a faded look and an ancient, yellowish complexion'. It was, nevertheless, of interest to a passenger onboard, William Henry Jacques, who borrowed it to read. Jacques, a thoughtful, introspective and terminally ill young Cambridge graduate, considered the book 'distinctly' worth finishing and, on being asked by its author whether he found it interesting, replied 'Very much!'.

On this voyage Conrad also met his life-long friends Edward Sanderson and the writer John Galsworthy, who were returning from a fruitless expedition to Samoa in search of Robert Louis Stevenson. Galsworthy wrote in 1906 to the journalist and critic William Archer:

'My meeting with Conrad took place in March 1893 on the sailing ship "Torrens" in Adelaide Harbour. He was engaged on 'the weight of her burden' in other words 'stowing cargo' and what with heat worry and dirt had the air of a pirate. I who had come aboard to choose whether I should learn navigation (we made a voyage of two months together to Cape Town). Conrad's watches (he was first officer) were to me the gems of the voyage - if you know him as a raconteur you will understand. He had then with him the manuscript (reluctantly produced) of about half "Almayer's Folly."'

Galsworthy seemed more impressed with Conrad's ability to spin yarns than with his navigational skills and Conrad himself now truly felt as though the 'story-teller were being born into the body of a seaman'. He gave up his promising position with the *Torrens* and wasted little time in London before setting out to visit Bobrowski, who was by now very frail. He spent the late summer on the estate in Poland, once again glad to be cared for by his family as though he 'were a little child'. It must have been a wrench returning to London.

'There are moments when the mind slumbers, the months slip away, when hope itself seems dead. I am experiencing one of these periods.' Thus wrote Conrad to Marguerite from Gillingham Street in early November. He had no job, having decided to work on his novel which was not progressing well: 'It seems to me I have seen nothing, see nothing, and shall always see nothing. I could swear there is only the void outside of the walls of the room where I am writing these lines.' Conrad began to haunt the London Shipmasters' Society in Fenchurch Street, and now there was nothing for it but to plunge once again into the life of duty.

On 29 November, Conrad joined the *Adowa*, an iron steamer which planned to carry emigrants from France to Canada. After a sojourn in Victoria Dock, the ship arrived at Rouen on 4 December. Here she stagnated for over a month until it became clear that neither she nor its second mate would cross the Western Ocean. Conrad occupied the time working on the tenth chapter of his novel and sending Marguerite 'outpourings inspired by spirituous liquors sold at retail'. Eventually the ship returned to London, where Conrad signed off on 18 January 1894. The short voyage across the Channel was the last he would ever make as a professional sailor.

'Into the heart of an immense darkness'

Great Bridge at Rouen,
1896, painted by
Camille Pissarro
(1831–1903)

Bridgeman Art Library

❧ *'Mr Conrad knows how to write English...'*

'My uncle died on the 11th of this month, and it seems as if everything has died in me.' Conrad's few words to Marguerite, written on 18 February 1894, express the profound and bewildering grief he felt on learning that his greatest support in life was gone for ever. Bobrowski had acted as father, friend, adviser, banker and confessor to the infant, child, youth and man whom he had always regarded as more than a little wayward, but for whom he had always found great reserves of forgiveness and love.

In a 'struggle to the death', Conrad threw himself into the completion of *Almayer's Folly*. 'I begrudge each minute I spend away from the page', he told his aunt, enclosing with his letter a copy of the first page of the manuscript. A stay with Edward Sanderson at his father's school in the countryside helped to discipline progress and on 24 April, back in London, he was able to inform his aunt 'of the death of Mr Kaspar Almayer, which occurred this morning at 3 o'clock.' 'Since I woke this morning', he continued, 'it seems to me that I have buried a part of myself in the pages which lie here before my eyes. And yet I am - just a little - happy.'

Conrad had not finished the novel completely. He went back to make certain revisions which, it has been pointed out, stress the theme of paternal love; and there was, of course, only one person to whom the work could be dedicated - Tadeusz Bobrowski. Conrad sent the manuscript off to the London publisher Fisher Unwin in July. The novel was appraised by two readers, W. H. Chesson and Edward Garnett. The latter, who would become a stalwart supporter and friend, was an extremely able literary critic and gifted spotter of talent. He was intrigued by the 'strangeness of the tropical atmosphere' and the 'poetic realism' of Conrad's narrative. There was no need for the author's pre-paid, self-addressed envelope. Garnett advised his superiors to take the novel on. When Garnett met Conrad, ten years his senior, on 8 October, he remembered confronting 'a dark-haired man, short but extremely graceful in his nervous gestures, with brilliant eyes, now narrowed and penetrating, now soft and warm, with a manner alert yet caressing, whose speech was ingratiating, guarded and brusque turn by turn.'

The final stage of Conrad's extraordinary metamorphosis was complete. The sea was behind him; he was now officially an author. Yet despite Garnett's early recognition of his genius, for many years the writer's life would not be an easy one. It would be some twenty years before his literary talents commanded any degree of widespread respect. Conrad's dark, provocative vision of human fallibility uncompromisingly expressed in dense and difficult language did not appeal to the novel-reading public of the time. Macmillan published the American edition, and their begrudging reader left little doubt of his views in a report of 2 May 1895:

'Mr Conrad knows how to write English, and his work is true enough, I can fancy, in its scene and characters to the life; but it is a stagnant, half-savage, sordid life, which needs an artist instead of a photographer to make even picturesque. The wretched half-crazy, bankrupt Dutchman is the central figure of a profoundly depressing picture. Clever it is of a kind, certainly, but with a cheerless, unprofitable cleverness, from which I can conceive no pleasure to be got .'

Twenty-three years later Conrad, although famous, was still bemoaning precisely such misguided readings of his work. The novelist Hugh Walpole observed in his diary that during an interview Conrad 'cursed the public for not distinguishing between creation and photography'.

In April 1895 *Almayer's Folly* was published in England. A month later Conrad wrote to Edward Noble, an appreciative reader who was himself a sailor trying to write. Conrad's touching words of encouragement balance his own hopes and fears against this younger version of himself:

'why do you misjudge so blindly Your own personality? And why do You belittle Your own temperament. You have Your own distinct individuality that may - and in time will - appeal to hundreds, thousands or millions - as blind fate shall will it. And it is an individuality that will stand wear and tear that has resistance and power - while I shall be used up in [a] short and miserable splutter of dim flame.'

Conrad may have been uncertain about the likelihood of ever having a wide audience. But he could be sure, at least, of one reader. Jessie George, a pretty typist from an ordinary background, was introduced to Conrad in late 1894 by his friend Hope. The two established what, according to Jessie, was a 'strange friendship'. Conrad inscribed a copy of *Almayer's Folly* to the awestruck woman, some fifteen years younger than himself, and for the next few months flitted in and out of her life. The friendship slowly grew more intimate. Conrad was by now working on *An Outcast of the Islands* (drawing again upon his Eastern experiences) and would invite Jessie to read from the manuscript. She recalled the first such occasion: 'he sat a few feet from me, his compelling eyes fastened on my face. I was even then conscious of something restless in him, of a sort of inward fire that robbed me of nearly all my powers of speech. I read on, stumbling over the corrections that interlined the closely typed pages.' For her trouble, Jessie was rewarded with a ruby and pearl bracelet when he completed the book, probably a gift picked up during his Eastern travels.

After intense work and another brief stay at Champel, *An Outcast of the Islands* was published on 4 March 1896. Less than a week later Conrad posted a copy to his distant uncle, Karol Zagorski. In the covering letter he made an important announcement: 'I am getting married', he exclaimed, continuing amusingly, 'No one can be more surprised at it than myself. However, I am not frightened at all, for as you know, I am accustomed to an adventurous life and to facing terrible dangers, Moreover, I have to avow that my betrothed does not give the impression of being at all dangerous.' The pair had a curious engagement; Conrad proposed, almost as an afterthought, in London's National Gallery, pointing out that 'he had not very long to live and no intention of having children' As part of the hasty preparations for

Photographs of Conrad and Jessie in 1896, the year of their marriage.

Yale University Library

their unglamorous marriage, which took place in a Register Office on 24 March with Hope and Krieger as witnesses, he insisted cruelly that his future wife should burn the few letters he had written to her from Switzerland: 'he himself superintended the sacrifice', she sadly recalled. 'Not one escaped.'

Conrad, in fact, had many more years to live and throughout every one of them Jessie was a tremendous source of love and devotion. She also played no small part in the practical business of getting his novels written; her skills as a typist were invaluable to Conrad, especially as the rheumatism and arthritis which plagued him from early on became increasingly severe. The Conrads honeymooned 'in the rocky solitudes' of Isle-Grande, off the coast of Brittany. Conrad's motives in seeking out this isolated place were ambiguous. He was not sure whether he wished to 'conceal from people's eyes our happiness', or 'our stupidity'. Probably his choice of destination had little to do with the celebration or otherwise of marriage; in such a remote setting there could be no excuses not to concentrate on his writing. Here he wrote *An Outpost of Progress*, drawing upon his African memories and started the novels *The Rescue* and *The Nigger of the 'Narcissus'*.

The extraordinary and celebrated preface to *The Nigger of the 'Narcissus'* shows the extent to which Conrad was intensely preoccupied with the philosophy of creation:

> *'A work that aspires, however humbly, to the condition of art should carry its justification in every line. And art itself may be defined as a single-minded attempt to render the highest kind of justice to the visible universe, by bringing to light the truth, manifold and one, underlying its every aspect.'*

This truth was not, for Conrad, pretty or palatable; not something to be served up in a trifling tale for a reader's delectation. In a letter of 22 August to his publisher, Unwin, criticising just such a story, he wrote: 'Our captivity within the incomprehensible logic of accident is the only fact of the universe. From that reality flows deception and inspiration, error and faith, egoism and sacrifice, love and hate ... To produce a work of art a man must either know or feel that truth - even without knowing it.' One imagines that Jessie cannot have discovered much levity in her 'strange husband' by the time they returned from the island in late September 1896.

Conrad and Jessie moved out of London to a semi-detached villa in Stanford-le-Hope, near Gravesend, Essex. The house was close to that of Hope, with whom Conrad resumed yachting trips; the area was to be hauntingly evoked in the first few lines of *Heart of Darkness*:

> *'In the offing the sea and the sky were welded together without a joint, and in the luminous space the tanned sails of the barges drifting up with the tide seemed to stand still in red clusters of canvas sharply peaked, with gleams of varnished sprits. A haze rested on the low shores that ran out to sea in vanishing flatness. The air was dark above Gravesend, and farther back still seemed condensed into a mournful gloom, brooding motionless over the biggest, and the greatest, town on earth.'*

Conrad worked hard at finishing 'The Nigger of the Narcissus'. He wrote to the Zagorskis on the 20 December, 'I have been writing, writing endlessly - and now the sight of an inkwell and of a pen fill me with anger and horror; - but I go on writing!'. When the novel appeared a year later it received acclaim from discriminating literary critics. One heralded it as 'one of the most powerful and extraordinary books of the year'. The Conrads moved again, on 13 March 1897, to nearby Ivy Walls Farm, an Elizabethan house close enough to the Thames for Conrad to hear the familiar bells of the ships. He was by now working on *Tales of Unrest*, which eventually appeared in March 1898. Despite the fact that this collection had, at least in part, cost him a great deal 'in sheer toil, in temper, and in disillusionment' he had also managed to

William Blackwood, one of Conrad's earliest publishers.

National Portrait Gallery of Scotland

establish an encouraging and important relationship with Blackwood's Magazine and its Scottish editor, William Blackwood.

In the summer of 1897 Conrad received a letter, quite out of the blue, from Janina de Brunnow, whom he had first known (and possibly loved), as Janina Taube back in his childhood days in Cracow. In a letter to her of 2 October he summed up his situation:

> *'I married about 18 months ago and since then I have worked without interruption. I have acquired a certain reputation - a literary one - but the future is still uncertain because I am not a popular author and I shall probably never become one. That does not depress me in the least as I have never had any ambition to write for the all-powerful masses. I have no liking for democracy and democracy has no liking for me! I have gained the appreciation of a few chosen spirits and I do not doubt that I shall eventually create my own public - limited of course, but large enough for me to earn my living. I do not dream of making a fortune and anyway it is not something to be found in an ink well. However, I must confess that I dream of peace, of a little recognition and of devoting to Art the rest of a life that would be free from financial worries. Here you have chére Madam, the secret of my life.'*

Among the 'few chosen spirits' appreciative of Conrad were the internationally acclaimed Henry James, whom he first met in February 1897, the writer and critic H. G. Wells, who had favourably reviewed *An Outcast of the Islands*, Arthur Thomas Quiller-Couch, an academic and writer, and the flamboyant Scottish Nationalist Robert Bontine Cunninghame Graham, who would help and inspire him to write the epic *Nostromo*. Conrad's fervent letters to these men covered subjects literary, political, personal and philosophical. In a letter of 20 December, for example, Conrad explained to the 'idealist' R. B. Cunninghame Graham his own unremittingly nihilistic vision of the world:

> *'There is a - let us say - a machine. It evolved itself (I am severely scientific) out of a chaos of scraps of iron and behold! - it knits. I am horrified at the horrible work*

and stand appalled ... It knits us in and it knits us out, It has knitted time, space,

pain, death, corruption, despair and all the illusions - and nothing matters.'

Three days later he was writing from a completely different perspective, to Quiller-Couch about what he had hoped to achieve with *The Nigger of the 'Narcissus'*: 'it has been my desire to do for seamen what Millet ... has done for peasants... I am concerned for the men - and for the men only. It is a great relief and a great pleasure to know you've taken them up - for it is not to dismiss them at once as "brutes and ruffians" (see reviews).' Another new but bitterly short-lived literary friendship was

R. Cunninghame Graham, to whom Conrad wrote some of his most profound letters.

British Library
Add. MS 54781

the one he struck up in October 1897 with the young American novelist Stephen Crane. Crane died of tuberculosis in 1900 but many years later Conrad spoke of 'an abiding affection for that energetic, slight, fragile, intensely living and transient figure'.

On 17 January 1898 Jessie gave birth to her first child. Four days later Conrad mirthfully announced the news to his distant aunt Aniela Zagorska: 'The doctor reports that it is a magnificent boy. He has dark hair, enormous eyes - and looks like a monkey. What upsets me is that my wife maintains that he is also very much like me.' The child's name reflected Conrad's Polish and English nationalities: Alfred Borys Konrad Korzeniowski. During this year Conrad finished only three reviews and the short story 'Youth', which appeared in *Blackwood's Magazine* in September. The obligations and frustrations of parenthood no doubt took their toll but there were other factors too. The death of Karol Zagorski on 19 January touched him deeply. He wrote to the widowed Aniela on 12 April, telling her that for two months he had been 'quite unable to follow my thoughts or to write a couple of lines'. Financial necessities - pressing as ever - forced him to resume but tainted with such sad news from the old country, he felt unsure of his loyalties and resentful of his present position. 'And it is thus, with poignant grief in my heart', he confessed to her, 'that I write novels to amuse the English'. His disillusionment lay behind an ultimately fruitless September journey to Scotland in search of a ship.

Despite his miseries, the year was by no means unimportant for Conrad's literary development. He began 'Jim: A Sketch', which would burgeon into one of his masterpieces, *Lord Jim*, and at the end of the year, struck a new and terrible note with *Heart of Darkness*. He also made friends with Ford Madox Ford, a young writer who shared his high-minded literary approach and with whom he would collaborate on various works. Writing in 1931, Ford recalled that:

Above:

Ford Madox Ford, one of Conrad's most important literary friends, in uniform.

National Portrait Gallery

Opposite:

Aniela Zagorska and daughters.

Duke University

Conrad's introduction to Stephen Crane's 'Red Badge of Courage'

British Library Ashley MS 4792, f.2

> *'In those early days he still had a great deal of the master mariner about him. His characteristic attitude was that, with his hands in the pockets of his coat and his beard pointing at the horizon. He strode, with the rolling gait of the quarter-deck, into a room or on to a terrace ... he could in telling stories, in his dusky and affectionate tones and with his singular accent, make you see almost anything in the world.'*

Conrad and family moved again, on 26 October, to Pent Farm in Kent. The house, a short distance from the sea, and rented from Ford, had an immediate appeal. 'I found that I could not work in our old place', he wrote to Aniela, before describing his new surroundings:

> *'A road runs along the foot of the hills near the house - a very lonely and straight road, and along which (so it is whispered) old Lord Roxby - he died 80 years ago - rides at night in a four-in-hand driven by himself ... On the*

other side of the little garden stretches out quiet and waste land intersected by hedges and here and there stands an oak or a group of young ash trees. Three little villages are hidden among the hillocks and only the steeples of the churches can be seen. The colouring of the country presents brown and pale yellow tints - and in between, in the distance one can see the meadows, as green as emeralds.'

Pent Farm, Kent, where Conrad lived from 1898 to 1907 and wrote some of his greatest works.

Author's Photograph

William Blackwood published *Heart of Darkness* between February and April 1899. The author outlined the scope of the story to Blackwood himself in a letter written on the last day of 1898: 'The criminality of inefficiency and pure selfishness when tackling the civilizing work in Africa is a justifiable idea. The subject is of our time distinctly - though not topically treated. It is a story as much as my *Outpost of Progress* was but, so to speak 'takes in' more - is a little wider - is less concentrated upon individuals.'

The themes of Conrad's novel were, and indeed remain, wide and far-reaching. The story was written at white heat, from the heart. 'I don't start with an abstract notion. I start with definite images', Conrad wrote to R. B. Cunninghame Graham on 8 February 1899. Strangely galvanized by his idyllic surroundings, Conrad sought not 'to amuse the English' but, through a recapitulation of his own most terrible impressions, to shake them to the core. The more perspicacious critics took the point. Hugh Clifford of the *Spectator* wrote that 'never, beyond all question, has any writer till now succeeded in bringing the reason and ghastly reason of it all home to sheltered folk as does Mr Conrad in this wonderful, this magnificent, this terrible study'.

Just before Conrad finished *Heart of Darkness*, he learned that his *Tales of Unrest* had been given a prestigious award by *The Academy*, a literary periodical. He was

heartened by the critical recognition but had to give the £50 reward to Krieger, to whom he still owed a further £130. Ironically enough, *Tales of Unrest* had been dedicated to his old friend, with whom relations were now decidedly cool. Conrad was in dire financial straits; neither could Hope help him out, having himself lost money in a South African mine. Helped by Blackwood, Conrad pressed on. Acutely aware of his precarious position, he nevertheless felt compelled to continue writing. He explained to Sanderson on 12 October:

The village of Postling, the idyllic location of Pent Farm.

Author's Photograph

81

'it is a fool's business to write fiction for a living. It is a strange. The unreality of it seems to enter one's real life, penetrate into the bones, make the very heart beats pulsate illusions through the arteries. One's will becomes the slave of hallucinations, responds only to shadowy impulses, waits on imagination alone. A strange state, a trying experience, a kind of fiery trial of untruthfulness. And one goes through it with an exaltation as false as the rest of it. One goes through it - and there's nothing to show at the end. Nothing! Nothing Nothing!'

'The Human heart is vast enough to contain all the world.' A page from the manuscript of Lord Jim.

British Library
Ashley MS 4456, f.8

Despite the lack of financial reward and wide acclaim, by 19 January 1900 Conrad could inform Cunninghame Graham that 'in the fourteen months I've been at the Pent I've writen upwards of 100 000 words'. Seven months later he had finished *Lord Jim*, despite bouts of gout. From 20 July until 18 August, the Conrads and the Fords spent a working holiday in Brussels. It was not much of a break. 'I can't rope in a complete thought', Conrad wrote one week into it, 'I am exhausted mentally and very depressed'. To make matters worse, Borys fell seriously ill.

Shortly after his return to England, Conrad became a client of the esteemed literary agent J. B. Pinker, who for the next ten years, despite their often tetchy relations, would provide tremendous moral and financial support. He had enough respect for Conrad's intellectual integrity to allow him to continue in a vein not likely to benefit either of them very much financially. And despite his continued 'irritability, weakness, pain', proper representation would allow Conrad to adopt a more robustly confident attitude towards his endeavours. 'I am not ashamed of my undertaking', he wrote on 14 February 1901 to a fellow Pole and namesake, 'as the path I have chosen is by no means an easy one - on the contrary, it is difficult and precarious - striving for recognition not by inventing plots, but by writing in a style which serves the truth as I see and feel it'.

By this time, Conrad had finished *Typhoon* and was preparing for hard work on the short stories 'Falk' and 'Amy Foster'. In addition to *Blackwood's Magazine*, he had found the *Illustrated London News* and *Pall Mall Magazine* willing to publish his work. *The Inheritors*, on which he had worked with Ford, appeared in June. Another collaboration, *Romance*, was finished in March 1902. Ford recalled that 'the process of digging out words in the same room with Conrad was exhausting'; but a reader at Macmillan left little doubt as to who, in his opinion, was the greater writer:

'This is one of the longest stories I have ever read. It is long by nature (upwards of 450 pages) and doubly long by art - by the affectations of the style, the extraordinary minuteness of the details, and the variety, complexity, and breathlessness of the situations. I do not remember these defects in Mr Conrad's early stories - his later ones I could never get through with - and I suspect his partner must be in great measure responsible for them.'

A manuscript page from Romance.

British Library
Ashley 5760

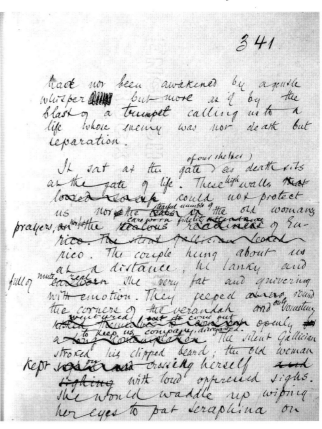

The reader, while acknowledging 'the necessary amount of love interest', 'good local colour' and 'clever scene painting', closes his report with an acute if depressing summary of Conrad's literary position: 'He is always praised by the reviewers, but I do not feel so sure that he is proportionately read by the public.' In his opinion, the 'extravagance' and 'affectation' of *Romance*, 'would not necessarily keep readers from it here, but they might among a less advanced public, unless

ROYAL LITERARY FUND.

£300 granted Wraxatens

Application on behalf of an Author.

Christian Name and Surname, in words at length, of the person for whom relief is sought.	Conrad, Joseph
Profession, University, or other Titles.	formerly, Master in the Merchant Service, now novelist
Age.	47
Present Residence.	Pent Farm, Stanford, near Hythe Kent
Whether Single or Married; and, if Married, or having been so, and having a Family, the Number, respective Ages, and Circumstances of the Children.	Wife & one Son. Two of his nieces Educates & him
If relieved before by the Royal Literary Fund; and if so, how often, and to what amount on each occasion?	No
Present Means of Support.	Literature
Cause of Distress.	Slowness of composition and want of public appreciation

TITLES OF PUBLISHED WORKS, in full. To be continued, if necessary, on the 2nd page.	No. of Vols.	Size.	Place of Publication.	Date of Publication.
Almayer's Folly	1		London	1895
An Outcast of the Islands	1		do.	1896
The Nigger of the Narcissus	1		do.	1897
Tales of Unrest	1		do.	1898
Lord Jim	1		do.	1900
et. et.				

Dated this 17th day of June 1902

(Signature of Member of Committee.) Edmund Gosse

the authors' names are of a sufficient weight to ensure an audience.'

After *Romance*, which he himself considered 'something of no importance', but which inspired the admission that 'Ford has become a habit', Conrad turned his attention to a short story 'The End of the Tether'.

Three months into his writing, disaster struck. On 24 June he wrote to Ford:

'Last night the lamp exploded here and before I could run back into the room the whole round table was in a blaze, books, cigarettes, MS - alas. The whole 2d part of End of Tether, ready to go to E'gh. The whole! The fire ran in streams and Jess and I threw blankets and danced around on them; the blaze in the window was remarked in Postling then all was over but the horrid stink ... This morning looking at the pile of charred paper - MS and typed copy - my head swam; it seemed to me the earth was turning backwards.'

Conrad neverthless decreed to 'buckle to' and the story was serialized in *Blackwood's Magazine* throughout the latter part of the year. His confidence and his resources were boosted immensely in July by a grant of £300 from the Royal Literary Fund, a long-established (still active) institution providing relief for authors in financial distress. Significantly, Conrad had not applied to the fund himself, but had been taken up as an important and urgent cause by writers of recognized status. Thus Edmund Gosse filled in the original application form, giving as the cause of distress 'slowness of composition and want of public appreciation'. Henry James acted as one of Conrad's sponsors, writing to Gosse on 26 June:

'The Nigger of the Narcissus is in my opinion the very finest & strongest picture of the sea and sea-life that our language possesses - the masterpiece in a whole great class; & Lord Jim runs it very close. When I think moreover that such completeness, such intensity of expression has been arrived at by a man not born to our speech, but who took it up with a singular courage, from

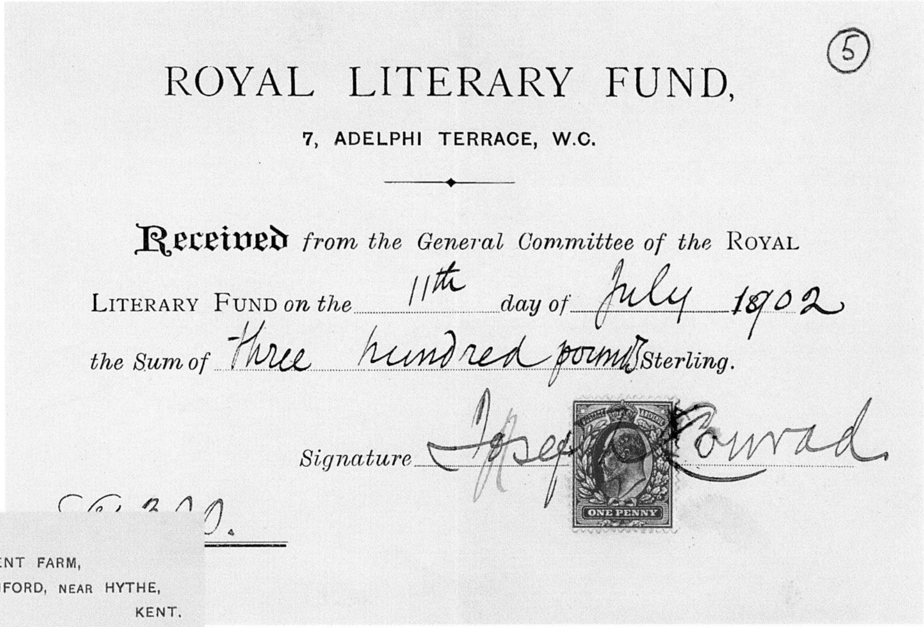

ROYAL LITERARY FUND,

7, ADELPHI TERRACE, W.C.

Received *from the General Committee of the* ROYAL LITERARY FUND *on the* 11th *day of* July 1902 *the Sum of* three hundred pounds *Sterling.*

Signature Joseph Conrad

£300.

STATION: SANDLING JUNCTION, S.E.R.

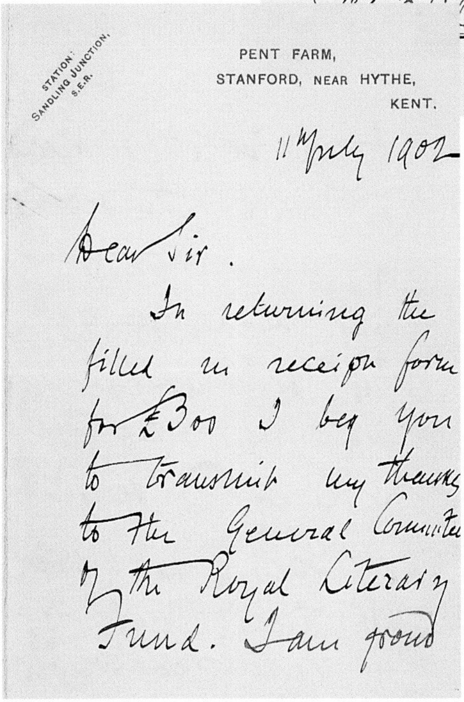

PENT FARM,
STANFORD, NEAR HYTHE,
KENT.

11th July 1902

Dear Sir.

In returning the filled in receipt form for £300 I beg you to transmit my thanks to the General Committee of the Royal Literary Fund. I am proud

to see stated black on white the grounds on which the grant was made — and this sentiment enters into my natural feeling of gratitude.

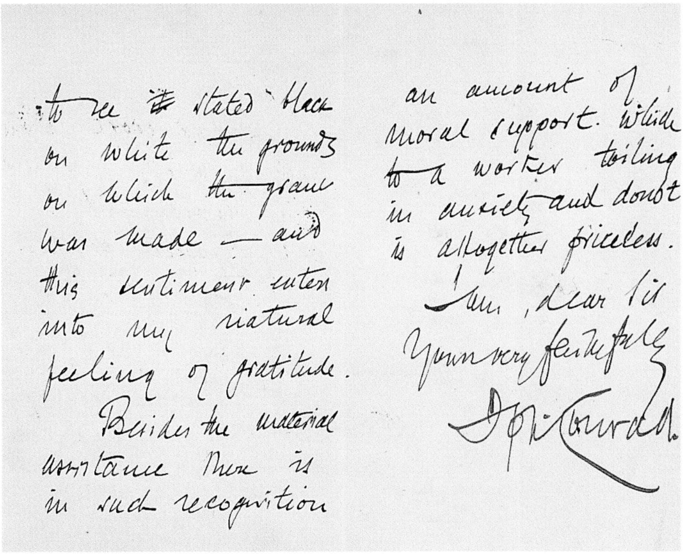

Besides the material assistance there is in such recognition an amount of moral support which to a worker toiling in anxiety and doubt is altogether priceless.

I am, dear Sir
Yours very faithfully
Jph Conrad.

necessity & sympathy, & has laboured at it heroically & devotedly, I am equally impressed with the fine persistence & the intrinsic success. Born a Pole & cast upon the waters, he has worked out an English style that is more than correct, that has quality & ingenuity. The case seems to me unique and worthy of recognition. Unhappily, to be very serious & subtle isn't one of the paths to fortune.'

Conrad's letter of thanks to the Royal Literary Fund and receipt for £300.

British Library Loan 96, case file 2629

*Henry James (right)
and J.M. Barrie.*

*Hulton Getty
Picture Collection*

On 11 July Conrad returned his filled in receipt form for the £300 along with a covering letter thanking the committee and informing it that: 'Besides the material assistance there is in such recognition an amount of moral support which to a writer toiling in anxiety and doubt is altogether priceless.' Conrad embarked next upon *Nostromo*, his epic account of the fortunes of a fictional South American country.

The two-year period of creation was not easy. Physically, Conrad suffered attacks of gout. Mentally, he vacillated between a sense of great confidence in the novel's destiny and one of almost total pessimism. On 22 August 1903 he wrote to Pinker: 'I have never worked so hard before - with so much anxiety. But the result is good. You know I take no credit to myself for what I do - and so I may judge my own performance. There is no mistake about this. You may take up a strong position when you offer it here. It is very genuine Conrad.' Yet by the end of the year he had written to the Polish historian Kazimierz Waliszewski, 'Am I achieving anything? I do not know - or rather, I know I am not ... I write with difficulty, slowly, crossing out constantly', concluding, 'What a foul profession!'.

Fate also played its hand in the novel's chequered progress. Another letter to Waliszewski of March 1904 paints a depressing picture:

'For a month now we have been involved in all sorts of unpleasantnesses. My poor wife fell and dislocated her knee. And so doctor, surgeon and masseur came into the picture. On top of this my bank failed and I found myself without bank, without money, without even a cheque book - an excruciating experience which still makes me shudder when I think of it.'

Jessie's fall rendered her lame for the rest of her years. In order to solve their immediate financial difficulties, Conrad turned his hand to a series of short projects for publication in newspapers and magazines. He announced cynically to H. G. Wells:

'I've started a series of sea sketches and have sent out P(inker) on the hunt to place them. This must save me. I've discovered that I can dictate that sort of bosh without effort at the rate of 3000 words in four hours. Fact! The only thing now is to sell it to a paper and then make a book of the rubbish. Hang!'

Conrad sold the loosely autobiographical sketches to various periodicals and

William Rothenstein's portrait of Conrad in 1903.

National Portrait Gallery

they eventually appeared in book form, in October 1906, as *The Mirror of the Sea*. Galsworthy's assessment of this was more generous than the author's own. He described it to Archer just before it appeared as 'a splendid thing written from the heart of a true seaman, and full of truth and life and beauty'. In an additional expedient, suggested to him by a new friend, Sidney Colvin, Keeper of Prints and Drawings at the British Museum, Conrad hastily cobbled together a single-act play, 'One Day More', based on the short story 'Tomorrow'.

The family had been staying in London, where Conrad could receive support from Ford. Conrad himself saw the strategy only as 'a sort of desperate move in the game I am playing with the shadow of destruction' and by the end of March they had returned to Pent. Extremely agitated and frantic to finish the novel but somehow unable to bring himself to

Two heavily revised pages from the manuscript of Nostromo.

British Library Ashley 463, f10-10v

do so, Conrad went to stay with Hope in Essex 'where I had to take off my brain that seemed to turn to water'. The days before he finally finished, at the end of August, passed in a confused haze. In a letter of 1 September to Galsworthy he remembered a nightmarish period, including a visit from the dentist, an episode of sleepwalking, '30 drops of chlorodyne', and the car journey to Hope's in which an unwary pedestrian was run over but, thankfully, 'only shaken'. In the last year of his life, Conrad wrote to the journalist Allan Monkshouse about the novel:

> *'My over anxiety, passing often into a weary restlessness, while writing that book, is responsible for a frequent clumsiness of expression. I can look back at that time now with a smile. Not only the youngsters have their illusions about the importance of this work, which are ridiculous and also a little touching. I was 46 - but as an author still young and I thought N a big undertaking.'*

Capel House,
Orlestone,
Nr Ashford.

19th June '18

Dear Mr Gosse

While I'm hunt for a decent copy of Rems proceeds (serious scouts are out) I've had a copy of Nostromo bound and beg you to give it the hospitality of your shelves. I have a great weakness for that work as my biggest creative effort. There are also other grounds for that special affection. This reprint (after 14 years) has got a bit of a preface of the autobiographical kind, on which perhaps you will cast an eye which I know to be friendly now as much as in the early days.

Believe me
Very sincerely yours
Joseph Conrad.

Despite the author's modest tone, *Nostromo* has been described (by Walter Allen) as 'the greatest novel in English of this century'. Few would now dismiss such a claim but Conrad enjoyed no praise on the book's appearance on 14 October 1904. It was, he wrote two years later, 'buried alive'.

Conrad's more immediate concern was with Jessie, who required an operation on her knee. Once this had been successfully, albeit painfully, undertaken, they set off on 13 January for warmer climes. 'I am sunk in a vaguely uneasy dream of visions - of innumerable tales that float in an atmosphere of voluptuously aching bones', Conrad wrote to Ford from the island of Capri on 9 May, continuing with a lurid description of local life before concluding 'it is a nightmare with the fear of the future thrown in'. The only good news came from home, and even then with a snag. Conrad had been awarded £500 by the Royal Bounty Fund. He was not, however, to have the money in one lump sum but piecemeal. This gave the embarrassing appearance, as he wrote to Gosse, of 'Conrad having to be saved from himself'.

'I have a great weakness for that work as my biggest creative effort'. A letter of 1918 from Conrad to Edward Gosse about Nostromo.

British Library Add. MS 70949, ff.566-566v.

Capri, where Conrad found himself 'sunk in a vaguely uneasy dream of visions - of innumerable tales that float in an atmosphere of voluptuously aching bones'.

Hulton Getty Picture Collection

The trip was not altogether unproductive, being beneficial to Jessie's health and allowing Conrad to work on *Chance*, the novel destined to finally bring him fame.

The return to Pent on 18 May 1905 was followed by a year working on *Chance* and various short stories, including 'Verloc', which grew into *The Secret Agent*, a London-based novel of anarchy, intrigue and murder. Health problems continued to hamper the family. On 31 October Conrad wrote to Ada Galsworthy that Jessie had suffered 'a violent fit of palpitation', symptomatic of 'nervous breakdown of a sort' and probably having something to do with the 'sameness of existence varied by nothing but anxiety during my fits of gout'. A month later, Borys was in hospital with scarlet fever. To be near him, his parents moved to Kennington in South London - a 'delectable neighbourhood' Conrad ironically informed Sidney Colvin.

Throughout their enforced stay in London, Conrad concentrated on his anarchist stories, which he found more profitable than 'the sea papers'. Once Borys had recovered enough to travel they set off for Montpellier. ''Tisn't a luxury. It's a necessity of life' Conrad wrote to William Rothenstein, the artist and socialite whom he had met when the latter painted his portrait. Conrad worked on 'Verloc' in the family's rooms on the top floor of an imposing hotel which had met both Jessie's medical requirements and those of the fragile Borys. Conrad's writing forged ahead and the break was altogether more successful than that in Capri had proved.

The Conrads returned to Pent on 14 April 1906 and a month later went to Winchelsea where Conrad collaborated on *The Nature of a Crime* with Ford, in whose

A page from Conrad's letter to Ford Madox Ford about Capri.

British Library
Ashley MS 2922, f.2

Left, centre and opposite page:

Conrad's letter of 8 August 1906 to Ford Madox Ford's wife Elsie announcing the birth of John.

British Library Ashley MS 2923, f24, 24v, 25, 25v

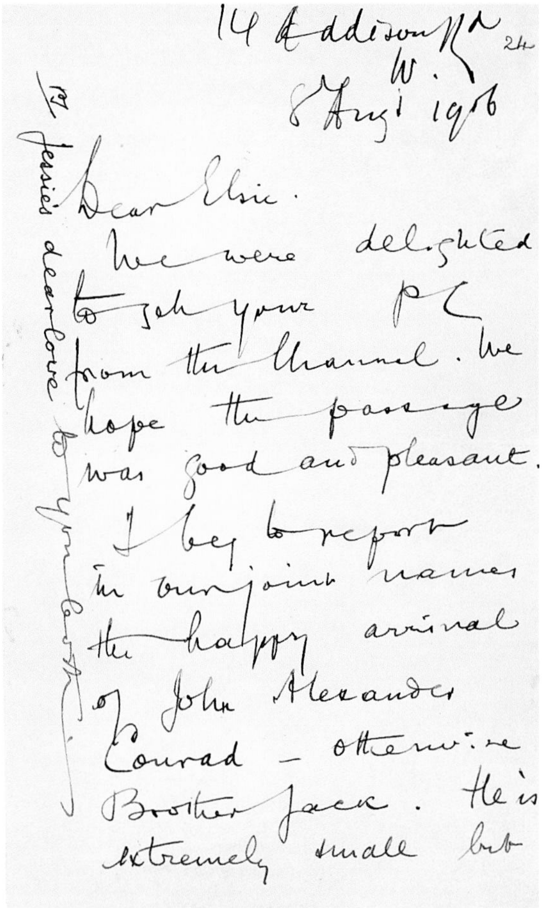

[handwritten letter reproduced]

magazine, *English Review*, it appeared three years later. The summer was spent in London, with Conrad preparing for the publication of *The Mirror of the Sea* and working intently on *The Secret Agent*. The story was partly based on the much-reported attempt of Martial Bourdin, fatal only to himself, to blow up the Greenwich Observatory on 15 February 1894. Conrad wrote to the publisher Algernon Methuen on 7 November 1906:

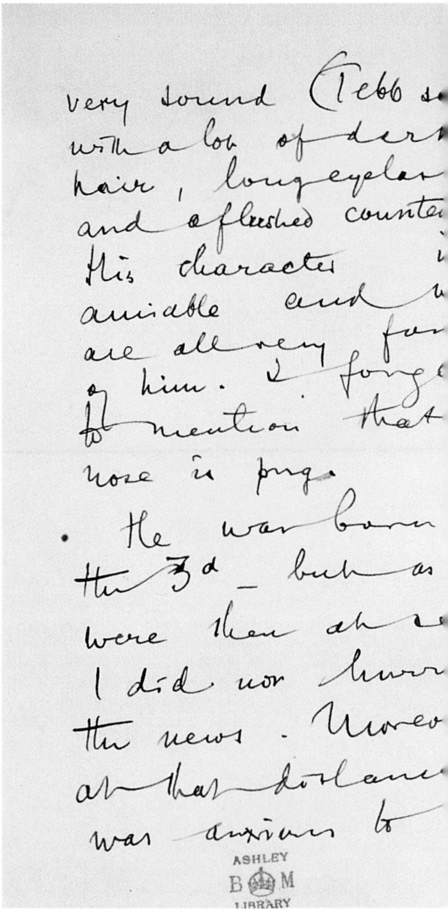

> 'I confess that in my eyes the story is a fairly successful (and sincere) piece of ironic treatment applied to a special subject ... And it is based on the inside knowledge of a certain event in the history of active anarchism. But otherwise it is purely a work of imagination. It has no social or philosophical intention. It is, I humbly hope, not devoid of artistic value. It may even have some moral significance. It is also Conrad's writing.'

The story, which among other things draws heavily upon Conrad's now extensive familiarity with London topography - 'not a drop of water in it - except the rain' - was serialized throughout the winter and appeared as a book in September 1907. It did not sell well. 'I suppose there is something in me that is unsympathetic to the general public ... Foreignness I suppose', he complained to Galsworthy on 6 January 1908.

Much had happened before then including the birth, as he wrote to Marguerite on 2 August 1906, of 'another boy, whose names are John Alexander Conrad, and for whom I ask a small place in your heart'. Borys, he continued, 'has already made a fair division of his toys and has also given him half of his dog - which is a proof of affection, I assure you'. If not ecstatic, the father at least seemed pleased with the new addition, feeling 'a good deal of friendship for him'. Following the pattern of previous winters, the four set off for Montpellier in December. Intended to be beneficial to their health, the trip saw both John and Borys fall seriously ill. In February Borys contracted measles, and his lungs became congested. The family moved on to Champel, all too familiar to Conrad.

Borys's illness became more serious, combining whooping cough (from which John now also suffered), pleurisy and rheumatic fever. Conrad, scarcely more capable than Jessie of ministering aid nevertheless did his best to nurse the boys. He wrote to Galsworthy in June of the terrible situation in which he was able only to 'move, talk, write in a sort of quiet nightmare'. John's gradual recovery gave his parents hope as Borys struggled on the brink of death throughout June. By the end of July the worst had passed and a relieved but impoverished Conrad sent to Pinker for desperately needed funds; he owed various doctors for at least eighty visits. On 12 August the family returned, exhausted, to Pent.

Domestic restlessness once again overcame Conrad and on 12 September 1907 the family moved to a new home near Luton. Conrad described Someries as 'a farmhouse of ample proportions and amiable respect'. With Borys now boarding at nearby St Gregory's school, Conrad launched into 'Razumov', which would become *Under Western Eyes*, and started 'Some Reminiscences', destined to emerge as *A Personal Record*. The strain he encountered with these works, particularly with respect to his dealings with Pinker and Ford, would contribute two years later to a shattering mental and physical collapse.

Conrad's time at Someries was productive enough and although fame was still a few years off, his reputation increased slowly but surely. He wrote his old friend Janina de Brunnow a touching, modest letter on 21 March 1908, in response to her request that he send her some of his books; ironically enough, he had been unable to secure first editions because the relatively few numbers issued had been snapped up by collectors. He elaborated upon his readership:

> '*I am read by the élite and also by very ordinary folk. One of my friends tells me that my books are in request in the public and popular libraries. The great middle class knows my name, but not my books. The painters also - I mean the young ones, the independent ones - also like my prose very much. In the literary world I have quite a name.*'

He now had enough of a name, in fact, to secure another grant, of £200, from the Royal Literary Fund. J.M. Barrie sent a letter of support as did Galsworthy, who noted of Conrad that 'his life ever since he became a writer has been one long struggle to keep his head above water ... he has been incessantly hampered by the illness of his family & himself'. H. G. Wells's laconic, wry letter of sponsorship perhaps betrays the fact that by this time a never particularly easy friendship had dwindled to a begrudging professional admiration: 'Conrad, that great artist, is hard up again. For such occasions the Royal Literary Fund exists. I am heartily in favour of supporting him.'

The gloominess of Someries led to yet another move, in February 1909, to the small village of Aldington in Kent. Although cramped, above a butcher's shop and disliked by Jessie, the new location meant that Conrad and Ford were practically neighbours. It seemed the ideal situation in which to continue a working relationship, with Conrad contributing instalments of his reminscences to Ford's *English Review*. But it was over just this arrangement that simmering tensions between the two finally boiled over. Although they later re-established cordial relations, the row between Conrad and Ford over a missed instalment effectively signalled the end of their intimate friendship. 'His conduct is impossible', Conrad wrote to Pinker on 4 August, 'He's a megalomaniac who imagines he is managing the universe ... A fierce and exasperated vanity is hidden under his calm manner which misleads people ... he's behaving like a spoilt kid - and not a nice kid either.'

Conrad's next argument was with his agent. Pinker was becoming increasingly frustrated with his client's inability to finish *Under Western Eyes*. Instead of focusing on this project, Conrad had diverted his energies into other work: first *A Personal Record*, then, in an attempt to raise money quickly for the treatment of an unwell maid, 'The Secret Sharer'. This vacillation infuriated the agent who felt every right to expect at least some return on his heavy investment. On 18 December 1909 he wrote to Conrad informing him that if he had not completed the novel within a fortnight he would withhold further payment for it. Conrad vowed to throw the manuscript into the fire if the threat were carried out.

Conrad eventually completed the novel and ventured from isolation into London on 27 January 1910 with the last part of the manuscript. A tremendous fracas ensued in Pinker's office. All the frustrations of the last two years - financial, mental, physical and literary - were vented upon the agent. Yet Conrad's rage sprung not so much from a resentment of Pinker's behaviour, as a deeply-wounding realisation of his own helpless dependence upon others. Between his telegram of 26 January to Pinker announcing his visit and the following March no letters appear to have survived. It was unlikely that he wrote any. Breaking his silence to Galsworthy in March, the reason becomes clear: 'I have stood up today for several minutes, the first time in six weeks ... I feel all crumpled up beyond all hope being ever smoothed out again.' The faltering syntax of his words bears out his admission 'that I find the writing of this, the greatest mental strain imaginable. A wretched state to be in'.

Jessie later recalled the terrible weeks of her husband's breakdown: 'He spoke all the time in Polish, but for a few fierce sentences against poor J. B. Pinker ... He seemed to breathe once when he should have done at least a dozen times, a cold heavy sweat came over him, and he lay on his back, faintly murmuring the words of the burial service.' She informed David Meldrum, one of Blackwood's literary advisers, that:

'Poor Conrad is very ill and Dr Hackney says it will be a long time before he is fit for anything requiring mental exertion ... There is the M.S. complete but uncorrected and his fierce refusal to let even I touch it. It lays on a table at the foot of his bed and he lives mixed up in the scenes and holds converse with the characters.'

Conrad's closest friends all rallied around to help during his gradual recovery. Jessie devoted herself to his care. Robert Garnett, Edward's brother, took over his legal and financial affairs and Galsworthy gave him support without which, Conrad acknowledged, 'I would have perished materially and morally too'. Pinker, although initially cautious, accepted a deal whereby Conrad would be paid four pounds per thousand words written. Their friendship picked up again, growing stronger than ever before. Conrad would never forget Pinker's faith in him during this period. He wrote to a friend in 1916: 'Our relations are by no means those of client and agent. And I will tell you why. It is because those books which, people say, are an asset of

English Literature owe their existence to Mr Pinker as much as to me ... he has seen me through periods of unproductiveness through illness through all sorts of troubles.' Borys proved a tremendous help too. So often nursed through illness by his father, he now gathered up and arranged six-hundred 'all unnumbered and considerably shuffled' pages of manuscript. Still confined to his bed and only able to work for short bursts, Conrad nevertheless set to his revisions.

'Apparently I nearly died of it', wrote Conrad of his illness to the translator Henry Durand Davray, before announcing triumphantly that 'I have been back at work for eight days, and I'm coming out of it fairly well'. A fortnight later he confided to Galsworthy that 'I am ... coming back to the world ... there is a sort of confidence'. *Under Western Eyes* was finally completed on 11 May 1910, marking for many the close of Conrad's most brilliant period of creativity. Yet his new confidence was not entirely unwarranted. In some ways, at least, he was emerging into an altogether brighter future.

The cottage at Aldington, Kent, where Conrad suffered a complete nervous breakdown. Beyond the upstairs window was Conrad's bedroom.

Author's Photograph

'strength, genius, thoughts, achievements, simple hearts...'

'To get away from this hole here is my ardent wish. We have found a home in the woods within 4 1/2 miles. It is picturesque and roomy. I must have space and silence - silence! I shall get that last there if anywhere outside the grave - which has no space.' Thus the convalescing Conrad announced his discovery of Capel House to William Rothenstein in May 1910. The farmhouse, set in an orchard, would serve as the family home for the next nine years. Conrad enjoyed the remoteness of the house which, nevertheless, saw a steady stream of distinguished visitors including, in 1913, the philosopher Bertrand Russell. 'It seems to me that I talked all the time with fatuous egotism', he wrote to Russell after their meeting, 'yet somewhere I had at the back of my brain the conviction that you would understand my unusual talkativeness.' For his part, Russell recalled delving 'through layer after layer of what was superficial, till we gradually both reached the central fire'.

At Capel, Conrad could enjoy long periods of blithe domesticity. In his memoirs, John recalled some of the stranger forms of relaxation taken by his

father in the house and its grounds. One involved summer expeditions to the orchard with the gardener, an expert in the macabre detonation of wasp nests:

> *'To "take" the nest Mr Knight produced a length of gas pipe ... with a cap on one end, with a small touch hole. This was filled with gunpowder and a length of fuse stuck into the touch hole. The open end of the pipe was pushed down into the nest and the fuse lit while everyone stood well away to one side and waited for the dull 'bumph' as the pipe was blown about four feet from the hole. Mr Knight then dug up the nest just to make 'sairtin' that all the occupants had been exterminated.'*

Less destructive pursuits included the building, with John, of complex Meccano models, some of which Conrad kept for a while in his own study, 'so that he could have a good look'. As the collection grew in sophistication (it had been started by the French novelist André Gide, a new and influential friend), Conrad's occasional shopping expeditions to London began to include the purchase of miniature steam engines. 'His knowledge', remembered John (later an architect), 'was very extensive and he spent a long time operating the throttle valve and adjusting the timing'.

John doubted whether Jessie had been consulted about these engines 'or about the smell and noise in which she was expected to type my father's manuscripts'. For between these curiously boyish diversions Conrad pushed on with his writing. *Under Western Eyes* had been finished before the move to Capel, appearing in the *English Review* throughout 1911 and as a single volume on 5 October. Various short stories were completed throughout 1910, and on 29 April 1911 Conrad resumed *Chance*. The work now took place in a healthier financial context. On 9 August 1910 Conrad was awarded an annual civil list pension of £100, and a year later the wealthy American collector John Quinn offered to buy various manuscripts, including that of *Under Western Eyes*.

While Conrad coached John on the intricacies of engines and mechanical structures, Borys aspired to a career which he hoped would make his father proud. On 22 September 1911 Conrad took his son to join *H. M. S. Worcester* as a cadet.

Never robust, Borys had recently suffered a deterioration in his eyesight, forcing him to wear glasses. This fact made his rather studious appearance on the gangway of the ship all the more poignant to a man who knew only too well the physical demands of sea-life. The next day he described their parting to Galsworthy:

> *'Poor Mons. B looked to me a very small and lonely figure on that enormous deck in that big crowd where he didn't know a single soul. It is an immense change for him. Yes. He did look a small boy. I couldn't make up my mind to leave him and at last I made rather a bolt of it. I can't get him out of my eyes.'*

The anxious father need not have been so concerned. When Borys left the ship in April 1914 he did so with a first class certificate, both in school work and seamanship.

Conrad's popularity at last began to grow. In France and Poland he was increasingly esteemed, while in America the publishing house of Doubleday launched a concerted publicity campaign. The company backed him as an author fit for inclusion in literature syllabi, distributed photographs and played upon his unusual past. By June 1914, the author was known widely enough to warrant the publication of the first biography. Conrad had met the author Richard Curle, a Scottish traveller, critic and collector, in London some two years previously in the Mont Blanc restaurant in Soho and they had subsequently become close friends. Curle had already written about *Nostromo* and would go on to enhance and enshrine Conrad's reputation in numerous other studies.

Curle's biography was timely. *Chance* had been published after frustrating delays (the first draft had been completed two years previously), on 8 January in England and 26 March in the United States. Not now generally thought to be a great work, it nevertheless quickly became a best-seller in both countries. Like Byron, Conrad at long last awoke to find himself famous. The youth who all those years ago made a 'standing jump out of his racial surroundings and associations' had, at the age of fifty-eight, finally landed. And it was back to those surroundings and associations that he now felt drawn. Conrad had last been to Poland in 1893. He had not seen Cracow for forty years. On 25 July 1914 the man now proud 'of infinitely dear and close ties ... of work done, of words written, of friendships secured' set off from Liverpool Street Station with his family, anticipating a journey which would not be so much 'a progress' as a 'retracing of footsteps on the road of life'.

The four embarked for Hamburg from Harwich, the dominance of steam vessels on the voyage causing the former master mariner to consider 'the great change of sea life since my time'. After a long train journey, the family arrived in Cracow on 28 July to the news that war had broken out between Austria-Hungary and Serbia. That fact and the lateness of the hour did not deter Conrad from walking out in the city with Borys. Against the backdrop of an impending international crisis, the 'coldly illuminated and dumb emptiness' of the streets soon summoned painful memories of his miserable childhood and his father's last illness. He returned, jaded, with Borys to the hotel:

> *'It seemed to me that if I remained longer there in that narrow street I should become the helpless prey of the Shadows I had called up. They were crowding upon me, enigmatic and insistent in their clinging air of the grave that tasted of dust and of the bitter vanity of old hopes.'*

As Europe slid further into war Conrad left the past behind and focused on the need 'to get my party out of the way of eventual shells'. On 2 August they headed for Zakopane, a resort some sixty miles away in the mountains, on the last civilian train out of Cracow. Two days later Britain and Germany were at war and, as a British subject, Conrad ran the risk of being impounded by the Austrian forces. For the next two months the family sheltered with Aniela Zagorska and her daughters, Karol and Aniela. During a time he described as 'wonderful' and 'poignant', 'tragic' and 'beastly', Conrad took the opportunity to broaden his knowledge of the Polish literary scene by making contact with the many writers and intellectuals gathered in the resort.

On 7 October, Conrad thought the time right to make a dash for home. With the help of his relatives, a new friend, Teodor Kosch, and the American ambassador, Frederick Penfield (to whom, appropriately enough, *The Rescue* was later dedicated), he managed to secure permission to travel to Italy. The journey was fraught with

risks for the fugitives, among them the need to avoid the cholera rife among the many wounded soldiers they encountered. They spent a short time in Vienna, managing to make Italy just before the Germans issued an order that they should be detained. From Genoa they took a Dutch mail steamer bound for England. A year later, in his essay 'Poland Revisited', Conrad recalled the sombre return aboard the *Vondel*:

'*As our ship's head swung into the estuary of the Thames, a deep, yet faint, concussion passed through the air, a shock rather than a sound, which missing my ear found its way straight into my heart. Turning instinctively to look at my boys, I happened to meet my wife's eyes. She also had felt profoundly, coming from far across the grey distances of the sea, the faint boom of the big guns at work on the coast of Flanders - shaping the future.*'

That ominous future would before long involve his eldest son. Although in June 1915 he and his father journeyed North to sort out a place at Sheffield University, by the autumn Borys had joined the army and in February 1916 was on his way to France. A gloom fell upon Capel; Conrad wrote anxiously to other parents in the same position, including both Pinker and Sanderson. Grace Willard, a friend who played a part in decorating the Conrads' homes, remembered a particularly moving occasion:

'*It was during the dark days of the war and for a torturing interval Conrad had had no news whatever of his son at the front. I had been at Capel House ... and was going back to London. Hunting up Conrad to say goodbye I saw him in his boy's room looking at the books, boyish books, taking one down and turning over the leaves, taking down another - as if it comforted him just to touch them. His hands trembled, his face was haggard with suspense and grief.*'

Borys survived the war, albeit as a victim of gassing and shell shock. Conrad and Jessie had their own battles to fight - the former with the old enemies of gout and depression and the latter with lameness. There were, nevertheless, moments of light. They had become acquainted, for instance, with Jane Anderson, a charismatic and beautiful American short story writer and war correspondent destined for a somewhat notorious future involving Hollywood, the Parisian underworld, fascism, imprisonment and alleged treason. She brought colour and vivacity into the day-to-day routine at Capel and there has been speculation that she may even have had an affair with her host. 'She is seeking to to get herself adopted as our big daughter and is succeeding fairly', Conrad informed Curle. 'To put it shortly she's quite yum-yum.'

Conrad himself contributed to the war effort. Duties carried out on behalf of the Admiralty included visits to naval bases throughout the land and a voyage aboard the submarine hunter *H. M. S. Ready* which, as he wrote to Pinker, 'will last 14 days - or, if it comes to that, to the end of life'. Neither was the plight of his old country forgotten. He submitted a paper to the Foreign Office setting out his views on Poland's future and, no doubt remembering his own life of exile, helped to raise funds for her refugees.

Conrad's most significant works of fiction during the war were *Victory* (probably the best-known of his mature works), started in 1912, *Within the Tides* and *The Shadow-Line*, which he dedicated 'to Borys and all the others who like himself have crossed in early youth the shadow-line of their generation'. He also threw his

9.   12

(which let me *confess here* in a white sheet I repaid by the basest
ingratitude) I have been permitted during the war to renew my contact
with the British seamen of the Merchant Service.   It is to their gener-
osity in recognising me, under the shore rust of twenty-five years, for
one of themselves that I owe one of the deepest emotions of my life, *Never*
for a moment did I feel amongst them like an idle wandering ghost
from a distant past.   They talked to me seriously, openly, and with professional precision, of facts, events and implements of which I had never
heard in my time; but the hands I grasped were like the hands of the generation which *had* trained my youth and is now no more.   I recognised the
character of their glances, the accent of their voices.   Their *moving tales*
tales of modern instances were presented to me with that *peculiar* turn of mind
flavoured by the inherited humour and sagacity of the sea.   I
don't know what the seaman of the future will be like.   He may have to
live all his days with a telephone tied up to his head and bristle all
over with scientific antennae like a figure in a fantastic tale.   But he
will always be the man revealed to us lately, immutable in his slight
variations like the closed path of *our* planet on which he must find his
exact position once, at the very least, in every twenty-four hours.

energies into the new possibilities offered by film, working on a version of 'Gaspar Ruiz' (about which he was somewhat bashful and which never saw the light of day) and negotiating with Pinker screen rights for earlier books. Indeed, it has recently been pointed out that later in life it was not so much the success of *Chance* which changed Conrad's financial situation for the better as the very considerable amounts of money he received from Hollywood.

By the end of the war Conrad's financial position was secure and his literary reputation had been further bolstered by Hugh Walpole's literary study of 1916. In October 1919 the family moved for the last time, to Oswalds, an elegant and spacious Georgian house in the centre of the idyllic village of Bishopsbourne, near

Left:

A portrait of Conrad in 1916.
by William Rothenstein.

National Portrait Gallery

Below:

Conrad expresses his remorse to T. J. Wise at having sold his manuscripts to the American collector Quinn - who later resold them at a huge profit.

British Library
Ashley MS 2953, ff.56-56v

Following pages:

A furious letter written to the journalist William Archer, showing Conrad's sensitivity to questions of his reputation.

British Library
Ashley MS 45291, ff. 51-51v

Oswalds today (in private ownership).

Author's Photograph

A letter to T.J. Wise on the manuscript of a film play on offer to him at 100 guineas

British Library
Ashley MS 2953 ff.35-35v

107

Private

4 C Hyde Park Mansions,
N. W. 1.
July 10th, 1918.

My dear Archer

I have your letter dated from Wellington House. I don't know what is the Department occupying that address, an ignorance which I share with 95 per cent of the subjects of the Crown. You make also a point of explaining to me that I wouldn't be eating your dinner but a dinner offered by a Department. As a matter of fact I would much sooner dine with you than with the best of Departments, but I can't accept an invitation from a Department Unknown to dine with one or two (!) Americans whose name (or names) are withheld from me.

You really cannot expect me to come to a dinner of that sort like an imbecile without even knowing whom I am going to meet. No personal distinction, even as great as yours, no exalted official position, and not even a close intimacy of many years gives a man the right to send out such an invitation. I wonder whether you would have

asked in such terms a barrister of any standing, or a doctor, or a clergyman. I very much doubt it. "One or two Americans!" I am sixty. I have 25 years of honest literary work behind me and it is highly improper for a Department to address me in this manner as if I were a youngster who ought to be glad of any sort of notice being taken of him.

On the other hand it is very easy to leave Joseph Conrad alone. He doesn't thirst for that sort of recognition. As to the distinguished Americans whose name you don't think worth while to communicate to me, if they really do want to meet Joseph Conrad they must find some other way. It wouldn't be very difficult.

Believe me
very faithfully yours
Joseph Conrad.

Canterbury. Grace Willard later wrote about everyday life there. Conrad, increasingly wary of towns and crowds and afflicted by gout more than ever, had gained the reputation of a recluse, yet 'his time, his interest, his house and purse, too, if need be were yielded to those whom he liked, believed in and whom he felt that he might help'. Oswalds, with its long views of elm meadows, 'became a Mecca for bookish travellers from America and the Continent, and the the week-end rendezvous of a small, exclusive coterie of literary London'.

Jessie, despite her own increasingly painful condition (for which further operations were required), 'contributed the magic oil necessary to running happily the household of a genius'. It was Jessie who now helped Conrad to organise sales of his manuscript material to another collector. This was Thomas James Wise, a prosperous bibliophile who paid Conrad well for items to augment his extraordinarily rich collection of Ashley manuscripts and fine books, now in the British Library. Conrad wished he had known Wise earlier when, close to the end of his life, he had to endure John Quinn making a ten-fold profit from the re-sale of his manuscripts at a sensational auction in New York.

Conrad occasionally ventured out of his retreat. He had long had a passion for cars and now had the money to buy a powerful Cadillac. Willard remembered her friend at the wheel: 'It was an experience not without a thrill of peril for others. But Conrad enjoyed it. He drove fast, rather

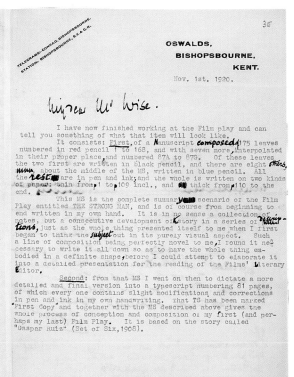

fantastically, but with complete joy. Now and then he would shout strange things in Polish to deliberate hens or silly Kentish sheep. Simple things amused him.'

1919 saw the publication of *The Arrow of Gold*, a novel looking back, rather fancifully, upon the author's early experiences in Marseilles. The following year saw the start of *Suspense*, of which Conrad apparently told Hugh Walpole: 'Of course, *mon cher*, it is not very good. I did my best work long ago.' *The Rescue* also appeared after its extraordinary gestation. Conrad had taken it up again in 1918, having set it aside twenty years before. 'As I moved slowly towards the abandoned body of the tale', he wrote in the Author's Note, 'it loomed up big amongst the glittering shallows of the coast, lonely but not forbidding'. Among other projects of 1920, Conrad wrote a memorandum to advise the Ocean Ship Company of Liverpool on the building of a training ship for boys of the Merchant Marine.

In January 1921 Conrad and Jessie went to Ajaccio in Corsica for the benefit of their health. The trip was not a great success. Conrad reported to Karola Zagorska that, although Jessie 'likes Corsica ... walks about with a stick and looks well', he himself felt a 'moral depression which I cannot shake off'. Back in Kent, he turned his attentions to translating a play, *The Book of Job*, by a Pole, Bruno Winawer. To do this meant putting aside work on *Suspense* and his limited collected edition for Heinemann, of which ten volumes had already appeared. Perhaps recognising his fading creative powers, he had decided to give a generous helping hand to a younger author. Despite the fact that Winawer liked the translation and Conrad himself thought it to be good, he did not hold out great hopes. He admitted to Winawer that 'my dramatized version of the novel *The Secret*

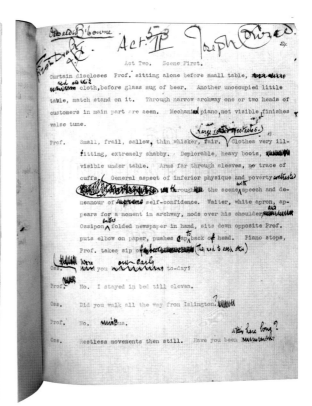

Agent has been wandering around the world for the last 15 months'. When Conrad's play was performed late in 1922 for a run of just nine days, he stoically informed Karola's older sister, Aniela, that the poor press reports had been given 'on the ground of defective stagecraft and absence of concentration of effect as a whole'.

By the end of 1921 Conrad had started work on his last complete novel, *The Rover* and seen *Notes on Lives and Letters* through the press. 1922 did not begin well. A month spent in bed with influenza and gout was concluded with the news that on 7 February Pinker had died suddenly in New York. 'It's a great sorrow to me', Conrad informed Winawer, 'Our friendship lasted for 22 years. He was 6 years younger than myself and I feel quite overpowered by this blow of fate'. Pinker's son took over the running of affairs - 'but it will never be the same', Conrad wrote to Karola. *The Rover* was completed at the end of June (appearing in December 1923) and *Suspense* moved ahead with characteristic difficulty. Conrad corresponded busily with Aniela about her translations of his works into Polish, but confided that his own

Above left:

Character notes for Conrad's translation of Book of Job *by a Polish author, Bruno Winawer.*

British Library Ashley MS 2941, f.3

Above right:

Conrad's stage adaptation of The Secret Agent *in manuscript.*

British Library Ashley MS 2946, f.54

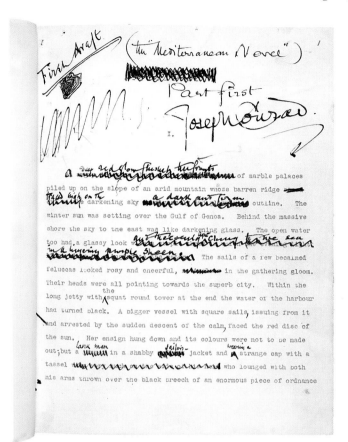

writing was desperately unforthcoming: 'I spend all my days sitting at my little table and by the evening I feel so tired that I no longer understand what I am reading.' Such evidence of sustained dedication, not only to his own but to a younger generation's literary efforts, serves as an antidote to Walpole's cruelly comic remark that 'Conrad never said anything very interesting in his last years; he was too preoccupied with money and gout. He was only really thrilling when he lost his temper and chattered and screamed like a monkey.'

For some years now Conrad had been the most famous living writer in England and America, and it was to America that he now planned a visit. Despite a healthy income, there never seemed enough money. He was going, as he wrote to Aniela, 'for my wife and children's sake - to improve the state of my affairs'. Conrad embarked from Glasgow upon the *Tuscania*, captained by David Bone whom he had met in Liverpool in 1919. He shared a cabin with Bone's brother Muirhead, an artist, who recalled the two captains sharing stories of the sea:

Opposite:
Joseph Conrad 1922.

Hulton Getty
Picture Collection

Above left:
The opening manuscript page of Conrad's last novel, 'Suspense'.

British Library
Ashley MS 2958, f. 1

Above Right:
Jessie and John at Oswalds, 1922.

British Library
Ashley MS 2953, f. 62

TELEGRAMS:- CONRAD, BRIDGE.
STATION:- BISHOPSBOURNE, S.E.& C.R.

47

OSWALDS,

BISHOPSBOURNE,

KENT.

March 26th. 1923.

Dear Mr Wise,

    I have finished my Crane article which consists
of 62 pages of manuscript, containing ~~between~~ 8351 words,
besides the title-page and the signature.

    Considering it relates to an American author about
whose memory there will be a certain stir made, I think I
could get for it $600 from Janvier. I wouldn't think of
taking it to America without asking you whether you would
care to have for, say, £110. I have not been in communi-
cation with anybody in America about it, my intention being,
unless you like to acquire it, to take it with me to the U.S.

    I know there will be inquiries for it and I expect
to be bitterly reproached for having left it in England.

I am now going over there on a dollar-
hunting expedition; and, though Messrs Doubleday may make arrangements for a few
semi-private lectures, there can't possibly be
much in it. Very lovely morning at all. I
have been making arrangements to
meet my expences and have reckoned on this
US to complete the minimum sum with which
I can venture on that journey. I need not tell
you that whether you secure this or not I shall
not engage myself over there for any more US. In
fact whatever happens I will ask you to treat this
matter as strictly between ourselves for a time.
Kindest regards. Sincerely yours J. Conrad

PS Should like to have the text of the letter (from Crane to me)
referred to in the MS, I will copy it in my own hand (it is very short) and join it
to the MS.

114

'*I remember his ... talking to David, in the captain's room, of all the sailing-ships and small tramp steamers of their mutual acquaintance and what had become of them. They ran over their names most lovingly; odd or to me very ordinary names which to these two seamen for some mystic and unfathomable reason seemed beautiful, exactly right and strangely appropriate, and David was able to tell Conrad most of their fates.*'

The *Tuscania* arrived in New York on 1 May 1923. Walter Tittle, an American portrait painter for whom Conrad had sat in England, was the first to greet him off the ship:

'*Royalty could not have been received with more distinction or enthusiasm, and Mr Conrad was amazed, I am sure, at the hordes of reporters, cameramen, reception committees and the public in general that greeted him. I smiled as*

*I left him moving slowly down the crowded pier, almost eclipsed by huge
bunches of American Beauty roses, all that his arms could hold. His unbelief
in his fame was being shattered!'*

The shy man who had lived for many years undisturbed among the orchards
and hop fields of Kent was, indeed, overwhelmed by the welcome which seemed to
him half-dream, half-nightmare. During his month-long visit he gave various talks,
including a lecture on 'Author and Cinematograph' and a reading on 10 May from
Victory. One member of the large audience felt sure that as he reached the novel's
tragic conclusion, the author was moved to tears by his own creation. Very happy to
be back at Oswalds, Conrad described his experience of America to Winawer:

*'I felt all the time like a man dans un avion [in an aeroplane], in a mist, in a
cloud, in a vapour of idealistic phraseology; I was lost, bewildered, amused -
but frightened as well. It was something that could not be caught either by eye
or hand. Obviously some power is hidden behind it - great power undoubtedly
- and certainly talkative. Its chatter reminds me of a well-trained parrot. It
makes me shiver! Tout cela est confié a Votre discretion [all that is in
confidence] as 1 I may be wrong and 2 I have feelings of great friendship
towards many people there.'*

The remaining months of 1923 brought different forms of anguish to Conrad,
among them Quinn's manuscript sale and the fact that Borys had married secretly, an
act for which his father forgave him only on the birth of a grandson in the new year.

Punished by heart problems and gout, physically exhausted and by his own
admission intellectually played out, even in the last year of his life Conrad displayed
the searching restlessness which characterized his whole life. He declined the formal
recognition, pomp and ceremony a knighthood would have brought, applied himself
to *Suspense* and embarked upon a quest for a new place to live. 'He must move',
wrote the sculptor Jacob Epstein for whom Conrad was sitting. 'He must find
another house. He would set out in his car. One step from the door to the sealed
vehicle to search for the new house.'

A telegram from Jessie to T. J. Wise announcing Conrad's death.

*British Library
Ashley MS 2953, f. 80*

It was while searching with Richard Curle on 2 August that Conrad suffered his second heart attack within a month. At Oswalds the following morning he succumbed to the third. Curle described the sad moments of his dying: 'His wife, lying powerless next door, heard a cry, "Here ..." as if a second word had been stifled, and a fall. People ran in: he had slipped, dead, on to the floor from his chair.' Jessie, the two sons, daughter-in-law and grandson turned to one another for comfort. Curle 'felt quite frozen'.

Conrad's funeral took place on 7 August in Canterbury. A small group attended a mass in St Thomas Roman Catholic Church and then made its way to the

cemetery on the edge of town. Friends and loved ones walked westward through streets festooned with flowers. The curiously comic and poignant fact that these were not for Conrad but the city's annual Cricket Week mattered little. Each had his or her memories of their remarkable friend. Each felt certain, like Muirhead Bone, that 'Centuries may come and go before anyone so gifted, so strange, and such a charming human being as Joseph Conrad comes this way again'.

selves for a time and observe the customs of the common people."

"Tell me, Attilio," Cosmo questioned, not widely but in a quiet almost confidential tone and laying his hand for the first time on the shoulder of that man only a little older than himself. "Tell me, what am I doing here?"

Attilio, the wanderer of the seas along the southern shores of the earth and the pupil of the hermit of the plains that lie under the constellation of the Southern sky, smiled in the dark, a faint friendly gleam of white teeth in an over-shadowed face. But all the answer he made was:

"Who would dare say now that our stars have not come together? Come to sit at the stern, signore I can find a rug to throw over a coil of rope for a seat. I am now the padrone of that felucca, but of course barring her appointed work you are entirely the master of her."

These words were said with a marked accent of politeness such as one uses for a courtesy formula. But he stopped for a moment on his way aft to point his finger on the deck.

"We have thrown a bit of canvas over him. Yes, that is the old man whose last bit of work was to steer a boat and strange to think perhaps it had been done for Italy."

"Where is his star now," said Cosmo after looking down in silence for a time.

"Signore, it should be out," said Attilio with studied precision intonation. "But who will miss it out of the sky?"

JOSEPH TEADOR CONRAD
KORZENIOWSKI
BORN DECEMBER 3ʳᵈ 1857
DIED AUGUST 3ʳᵈ 1924

SLEEP AFTER TOYLE, PORT AFTER STORMIE SEAS.
EASE AFTER WARRE, DEATH AFTER LIFE DOES GREATLY PLEASE.
SPENSER

JESSIE EMMELINE CONRAD
KORZENIOWSKA
BORN FEBRUARY 22ⁿᵈ 1873
DIED DECEMBER 6ᵀᴴ 1936

Opposite:

The last page of the manuscript of Suspense, upon which Conrad was working at his death.

British Library
Ashley MS 2958, f.330

Left:

Conrad's grave, shared by Jessie and other members of the family, in Canterbury cemetery.

JOSEPH CONRAD 1857-1924

~ *Chronology*

1857	3 December, birth of Jozef Teodor Konrad Korzeniowski at Berdyczow in Poland.
1861	Family move to Warsaw. Conrad's father imprisoned.
1862	Family in exile.
1865	Conrad's mother, Eva, dies.
1866	Conrad in Nowofastow with his uncle, Tadeusz Bobrowski.
1868	Conrad with his father in Lwow.
1869	Apollo dies in Cracow. Bobrowski appointed Conrad's guardian.
1873	Travels with Adam Pulman to Europe. Sent to school in Lwow.
1874	Sails as a passenger on the *Mont Blanc*.
1875-1876	Sails around the West Indies.
1878	Attempts suicide in Marseilles. Decides upon a career in the English Merchant Navy and sails for Lowestoft in England. Sails to Australia.
1879	Sails the Mediterranean.
1880	Passes exam as second mate. Sails to Australia.
1881	Begins seven years of voyages to the East. Has various lodgings in London.
1883	Sails as second mate on the *Palestine*, which catches fire off Sumatra and is abandoned. Reunited in Marienbad with Tadeusz.
1884	Passes First Mate's exam.
1886	Becomes a British subject and gains his Master's Certificate.
1887	Meets Almayer's inspiration, Charles Olmeijer, in Borneo.
1888	Sails to Singapore, Australia, Mauritius.
1889	Begins writing *Almayer's Folly* in Bessborough Gardens, London.
1890	Visits Tadeusz before departing for the Congo to take up a position aboard a river steamer, the *Roi des Belges*.
1891	Admitted with fever to the German Hospital in London and then recuperates at Champel near Geneva. Sails for Australia.

1893	In Rouen.
1894	Tadeusz dies. *Almayer's Folly* accepted by Fisher Unwin.
1895	*Almayer's Folly* published.
1896	Marries Jessie George. Begins *The Rescue* (published 23 years later) and 'The Nigger of the Narcissus'. Writes 'An Outpost of Progress', 'Idiots' and 'Lagoon'.

1897	Moves to Essex. Finishes *Nigger of the Narcissus*.
1898	*Tales of Unrest* published. Birth of Borys. Moves to Postling, Kent.
1899-1903	'The Blackwood period'. Publication of *Lord Jim* (1900), *The Inheritors, Youth* (1902), *Typhoon and Romance* (1903).
1904	Publication of *Nostromo*. Grant of £500 from the Royal Literary Fund.

1906	*The Mirror of the Sea* published. Birth of John. Trip to Montpellier and Geneva.
1907	Moves to Bedfordshire. *The Secret Agent* published.
1909	Moves to cramped quarters in Aldington, Kent.
1911	*Under Western Eyes* published.
1912	*A Personal Record* published.
1913	*Chance* published.

1914	Travels with family to Poland. Takes refuge in the Carpathians when war breaks out. Arrives back in England by the end of the year.
1915	*Victory* and *Within the Tides* published.
1917	*The Shadow-Line*, dedicated to Borys and others of his generation, published.

1918	Final move, to Bishopsbourne in Kent.
1919	*The Arrow of Gold* published.
1920	*The Rescue* published.
1921	Visits Corsica with Jessie. *Notes on Life and Letters* and a dramatisation of *The Secret Agent* published.

1923	*The Rover* and *Laughing Anne*, a play, published. Visits America.
1924	Sunday 3 August 8. 30 am, dies at home of a heart attack while working on his last novel, *Suspense*.

Sources and Acknowledgements

This book aims to provide a general introduction to the life of Joseph Conrad whilst offering new insights, information and illustrations. It could not have been written, however, without the work of those authors cited below to whose painstaking scholarship it owes a great debt. I would also like to thank Anne Young, Sally Brown, Stella Halkyard, Laurence Pordes, David Sutherland, the present owners of Conrad's houses and Susan Shaw.

Primary Sources

Published Autobiographical Sources
Conrad's letters were drawn from the five volumes published to date of the collected letters edited by F. Karl and L. Davies. Other letters, both to and from Conrad, were taken from Zdzislaw Najder's *Conrad's Polish Background: Letters to and from Polish Friends* (1964).

Conrad's two autobiographical works, *The Mirror of the Sea* (1906) and *A Personal Record* (1912) provide material for many of his quoted recollections. Also useful were his two collections of writings, *Notes on Life and Letters* (1921) and *Last Essays* (1926), as was Najder's 1978 edition of Conrad's Congo Diary.

Unpublished and Manuscript Sources
Wherever possible, but particularly in the illustrations, I have drawn upon the extensive holdings of original Joseph Conrad manuscripts in the British Library. These mostly form part of the Ashley Collection of Manuscripts, collected by T. J. Wise and purchased after his death in 1937. Other British Library manuscript sources cited or used include the Readers' Reports for *Almayer's Folly* and *Romance* from the Macmillan archive, Conrad's file in the Royal Literary Fund Archive and a cuttings book relating to exploration in the Belgian Congo which, like Galsworthy's letter of 1906 and Conrad's own, of 1918, to William Archer, form part of the Additional Series of Manuscripts. The letter of 1924 to Allan Monkshouse is at John Rylands Library, Manchester.

Other primary sources
Najder's *Conrad Under Familiar Eyes* (1983) provided a source for letters and other writings by members of Conrad's family and other Polish individuals. Martin Ray's *Joseph Conrad: Interviews and Recollections* (1990) provided a range of recollections and portraits by friends and acquaintances.

Secondary Sources

In addition to the works cited above, this book owes much to Najder's *Joseph Conrad: a Chronicle* (1983), Frederick Karl's *Joseph Conrad: the Three Lives* (1979) and to Norman Sherry's works *Conrad's Western World* (1971) and *Joseph Conrad* (1972). Useful information about Conrad's ships was found in Jerry Allen's *The Sea Years of Joseph Conrad* (1965). Other useful and significant studies are Richard Curle, *Joseph Conrad: A Study* (1914), Jean G Aubry, *Joseph Conrad: Life and Letters* (1927), Jessie Conrad, *Joseph Conrad and his Circle* (1935), Jocelyn Baines, *Joseph Conrad* (1960).

Photographic Acknowledgements

Unpublished letters of Joseph Conrad illustrated are reproduced by permission of the Trustees of the Joseph Conrad Estate. The author and publisher are also grateful to the following for permission to reproduce illustrations: The Bridgeman Art Library; Duke University, Rare Book, Manuscript and Special Collections Library; the Hulton Getty Picture Collection; the National Maritime Museum, London; the National Portrait Gallery, London; the National Portrait Gallery of Scotland; St Bartholomew's Hospital (The Royal Hospitals NHS Trust), London; and the Beinecke Rare Book and Manuscript Library, Yale University Library.

❧ *Index*

Front cover: Joseph Conrad (Hulton Getty Picture Collection); the manuscript of
Conrad's novel, *The Rescue* (British Library Ashley MS 4787);
Nightfall down the Thames, 1880, by John Atkinson Grimshaw
(1836 – 1893), (Bridgeman Art Library).

Back cover: Joseph Conrad (British Library Ashley MS 2953);
Pent Farm, Kent (Author's Photograph)

Half-title page: The *Torrens* (National Maritime Museum)

Frontispiece: Page from the manuscript of *Lord Jim.*
(British Library Ashley MS A456, f. 8.)

Contents spread: Lowestoft harbour (National Maritime Museum)

© 1999, in text, Chris Fletcher
© 1999, in illustrations, The British Library and other named copyright owners

Published in the United States of America by
Oxford University Press, Inc.
198 Madison Avenue
New York, NY 10016
Oxford is a registered trademark of Oxford University Press, Inc.

ISBN 0-19-521441-2

First published 1999 by The British Library, 96 Euston Road, London NW1 2DB

Designed and typeset by Crayon Design, Stoke Row, Henley-on-Thames
Colour origination by Crayon Design and Grafiscan, Verona
Printed in Hong Kong by South Sea International Press